Pragmatic Job Hunting

Using Project Management Concepts to Improve Job Hunting Efficiencies

Ayman Nassar
M.Sc. Eng. Mgmt., M.Sc. Elect. Eng
PMP, CSEP, CSSGB

Cover design and editing by Arif Kabir

ISBN-10 0-9823685-4-2
ISBN-13 978-0-9823685-4-1

Library of Congress Control Number: 2010900327

First Printing, May 2009 / Jumada Al-Awwal 1430
Intercontinental Networks Press, B1.0/C0.6
Clarksville, Maryland, United States of America

For direct sales please contact the publisher
Phone: 443.538.4121
Fax: 270.423.0419
Email: info@intercontinentalnetworks.com
Web: www.intercontinentalnetworks.com

Intercontinental Networks is a consulting and training firm, providing services in the domains of project management, systems engineering, enterprise architecture, product development, value proposition and systems leadership.

All praises to the Lord of the Universe, Allah (praises and glory to him), who perfected everything he created.

I write this book

To Doha, Yomna, Maryum, Jannah & Huda

To my younger brothers and sisters who are in college and high school, and to all my friends who lost their jobs in the recent downturn

To all those who are seeking to produce and contribute to the prosperity of the global economy and the goodness of the creation

Contents

LIST OF TABLES 7

LIST OF FIGURES 7

PREFACE 9

ACKNOWLEDGMENTS 13

FOREWORD 15

ABOUT THE AUTHOR 17

INTRODUCTION 19

Principles of Project Management 19

MANAGING YOUR JOB HUNTING 21

Defining Your Project – Job Hunt Possible 21
Cornerstones for Managing Your Job Hunt 22
Elements of Successful Job Hunting 23

JOB HUNTING LIFE CYCLE PHASES 25

Concept 26
Design 35
Implementation Phase 37
Deployment Phase 41
Disposal Phase 43

JOB HUNTING MANAGEMENT PROCESSES 47

Initiating the Job Hunt 47
Planning the Job Hunt 48
Executing the Job Hunt 50
Controlling the Job Hunt 51
Closing the Job Hunt 53

THE SCOPE OF THE JOB HUNT 55

Job Hunt Scope 56
Work Needed 57
Are We Focused? 59
Enforcing the Focus 59

JOB HUNT TIME UTILIZATION 61

Getting Active 61
Defining Resources 62
Working on a Schedule 64

JOB HUNT COSTS AND EXPENSES 65

Estimating and Budgeting 65
Controlling Expenses 67

QUALITY HUNTS 71

Get What You Expect 71
Control Quality of the Results 72

JOB HUNT SOLDIERS 75

Building Your Network Team 75
Managing Your Team 77

JOB HUNTING COMMUNICATIONS 79

How to Communicate 79
Using and Retrieving Information 80
Managing Your Stakeholders 82

PROJECT RISK MANAGEMENT 85

What Can Go Wrong 86
Qualifying the Risks 86
Prioritizing the Risks 87
Responding to Risks 88

ACRONYMS 89

BIBLIOGRAPHY 91

PRACTICE SHEETS 93

TIPS FOR THE RECESSION 109

While Still Employed 109
After Losing Your Job or After Graduation 110

A WORD ON INTERVIEWS 113

Phone Interviews 113
In-Person Interviews 113

NOTES 115

INDEX 121

List of Tables

Table 1 Definition and examples of project deliverables and artifacts. 20
Table 2 Key project management processes' artifacts and job hunting deliverables during the concept phase 29
Table 3 Inputs, outputs, tools and techniques for the concept phase of a job hunting project. 34
Table 4 Key project management processes' artifacts and job hunting deliverables during the design phase 36
Table 5 Main inputs, outputs, tools and technique for job hunting campaign design phase. 37
Table 6 Main inputs, outputs, tools and technique for job hunting implementation phase. 41
Table 7 Main inputs, outputs, tools and technique for job hunting deployment phase. 43
Table 8 Main inputs, outputs, tools and technique for job hunting disposal phase 45
Table 9 Initiation processes across the various project phases. 48
Table 10 Planning processes' focus and objectives across the various project phases. 50
Table 11 Execution processes' focus and objectives across the various project phases. 51
Table 12 Control processes' focus and objectives across the various project phases. 52
Table 13 Closing processes' focus and objectives across the various project phases. 54
Table 14 Job hunting team members and areas of contribution. 76

List of Figures

Figure 1 Job hunting project life cycle phases and process groups. 26
Figure 2 Job hunting project phases and key milestones 38

List of Tables

List of Figures

Preface

It wasn't too long ago when I was following the morning news, listening as the anchor reported on the increasingly rising rate of unemployment. It reminded me of the telecom bubble burst in the early 2000s. The burst happened right as I was starting a new product development company to supply wholesale telecom service providers with innovative network equipment. Investors would not even talk with us, and the focus at the time was shifting towards biotechnology, genetic engineering and life sciences. After an inspiring and challenging six months, I and the founding team decided to call it off. It was next to impossible to secure the $4 million needed for the first round of funding, and if we were to raise the capital, the follow-up rounds would have been more than just very risky.

I had learned a tremendous amount of knowledge and acquired unprecedented levels of experience in those six-months, compared to the rest of my career. I became an expert in starting companies, I recruited a board of professionals and scientists, I hired high school interns, entered into contracts with colleges to hire their students, traveled across the country to raise funds from successful technology angel investors in Silicon Valley, attended conferences, networked with chairmen of investment banks, and executives of the world's largest telecom service providers in the US and abroad. I learned about federal funding, proposal writing, state grants, even startup loans – although I would never sign up for one. I communicated with suppliers as far as Malaysia, and customers as far as France and Saudi Arabia. Through the bounties of God, I had a blast, it was all funded through seed money, and it was an experience of a lifetime. I was in control, I was learning, I was networking, I was growing professionally, and I was doing something I enjoyed and valued, even though I had no job, and was quickly depleting my savings to the point I almost had nothing left.

My plan had called for a six-month time investment into the startup; if we hit a wall, then I was to switch to either full-time employment or self-employed consulting. After some planning and strategic thinking I chose the self employment consulting route. Initially, I had to create new business leads and connections, and there was some time needed for things to pick up. I was invited to speak at some incubators, and developed some unique workshops in intellectual property, value proposition, product development and marketing.

It was in December of 2008 when I was chatting with a close friend of mine in the parking lot of the local masjid in my neighborhood as we were leaving the facility. He mentioned that he had lost his job in October. I was taken by surprise, for three months I would see this guy every week at least once or twice. We would talk on the phone almost every other day, and he would never mention that his job was eliminated as his employer gets acquired in a deal to save the energy conglomerate where he worked, from vanishing from the landscape of business. It wasn't too long after that when more people in the community started losing their jobs. A business analyst here, a construction engineer there, an SAP expert here, a business owner there, and the list just continued to grow.

I pondered what a job seeker can do to enhance his or her chance of landing a job in an environment where each month close to 500,000 Americans are losing their jobs. I started to remember my efforts in the past to secure employment during the IT downturn and how sour it was. I also recalled how I landed a job as an IT manager at an educational institution and because of that it was extremely difficult to get back into high technology and engineering organizations. I recall one recruiter even telling me, "You have an excellent resume, outstanding experience and accomplishments, but the IT management position is killing the whole positioning of your career". Although it was a senior professional position, and I was the head of IT operations and the data center at one of Maryland's largest community colleges, it did not flow naturally with my resume which for the past years illustrated a career path in product and service development for networking and telecom. Although I had presented some interesting accomplishments as part of that position, its lack of homogeneity with the rest of my technology experience in the areas of product development and service management seemed odd on paper and the eyes of recruiters.

I reflected on how difficult it would be today for any of those I know who lost their jobs, to get a new one, and if they did get a temporary one, how difficult it would be to move to one that would really interest them and match their career mission.

This book acts as a map to help those friends who are seeking to get back into the production line of the global workforce, and to those youngsters who are just coming out of high schools and colleges all over the world, hitting a wall called unemployment.

There are two main points to get out of this book. The first point is that you are not tied or stuck into traditional employment. You need a job, but it does not have to be a job as an employee; you could be self-employed, a contractor, a small business owner, or employed in some other way. The options are available, and you need to feel free and liberated to explore all the options, as long as they are legal and ethical. The second point is that to get where you dream to go, you need a plan, an organized approach and method. A well thought through plan will take you to your dream job. Dream big, plan smart, execute effectively and control wisely, you will get there with the will and support of your Creator.

These days are not those of haphazardly applying to jobs. We can't just see an advertisement in the papers or Internet, and apply without a clear solid structured plan that allows progress to be tracked and matched to our goals and objectives.

We live in times where the job hunting landscape is entirely different than a few years ago. We have technology gadgets and tools like never before. Internet social networking tools make our networks closer and less private. Outsourcing and globalization makes our competition fierce and challenging. Blogs and the Internet open new doors for opportunities and growth. Business approaches and models are more complex and bring challenges for perfection as well as opportunities for value creation. Job seekers need to be able to leverage the strengths of our societies' dynamics and overcome the challenges of the marketplace.

Ayman Nassar

Clarksville, Maryland

May 11th, 2009

Acknowledgments

إِنَّ اللَّهَ هُوَ الرَّزَّاقُ ذُو الْقُوَّةِ الْمَتِينُ

Quran (51:58)

Verily, indeed Allah (God) Himself is the All-Provider of all sustenance, and the All-Powerful, All-Strong.

Meaning of Quran parable 58, chapter 51 (51:58)

Nothing in this book would have been possible without the bounties of God and his compassion and mercy.

I thank my parents for the timeless hours they have spent on raising, teaching, caring and advising me. No matter what one says, I can never encompass all they did for me.

I thank Salah Elleithy for reviewing portions of the book and providing feedback. Although Salah might not be aware, his interactions and chats with me have been instrumental in motivating me to write this book. Appreciation goes to my friend and editor Arif Kabir for his support in editing this book and developing the art work.

Finally, I thank my readers for reaching out to pragmatic ways of landing that dream job. Enjoy the book and share what you enjoy with others.

A portion of proceeds of the sale of this book is donated to support youth leadership development programs, so please encourage others to buy a copy and purchase copies as a gift for recent graduates.

Foreword

The concepts of project management are becoming increasingly important as systems and processes around us become more complex. The body of knowledge of project management can be applied to many areas besides project management, such as problem solving, operations streamlining, performance audits and other areas. Additionally, project management perfectly compliments other technical management disciplines such as quality, product, engineering, services, and acquisition management.

This book provides a glimpse on applying project management concepts to job hunting. A daunting process in itself, complicated by the uncertainties in the current economic environment, job hunting requires new pragmatic approaches to ensure success.

There are many articles and books out there that discuss how to prepare for interviews, write good resumes, dress for interviews and network with others, so I do not attempt to address these tactical matters in this book. Instead, this book discusses the strategic steps needed to succeed in your job hunting project. It is your project, and you are the project manager, end user and main stakeholder, all in one. Other stakeholders are your family members and friends who will pitch in to pay your rent while you are unemployed.

Of course, it is assumed that you are networking with others like never before, that you have a professional voice mail message, email address and website URL. It is also expected that you are utilizing all resources available, whether it is a local library, former colleague, professional association, Linkedin, or your neighbor. Most importantly it is assumed that you are willing to be in the front seat and lead your project yourself as it is YOUR job hunt project and you have to lead it. So get ready to get the ball rolling.

About the Author

Ayman Nassar is a practitioner, consultant and trainer. He brings over 20 years of experience in project management, technology marketing, systems engineering, and product management.

Mr. Nassar has hands-on experience from dozens of projects worth more than $140 million in diverse domains such as telecom, IT, networking, data centers, software development, non-profit organizations, higher education and technology development.

He brings experience from managing complex multi-million dollar technology projects at Fortune 1000 businesses such as Ericsson, AT&T, Fujitsu, Acer and IBM, and several small and medium business size businesses and startups. He also offers mentoring and coaching in career development, job hunting & youth development. He has mentored professionals and students at IBM, Prince George's Community College ALANA program, MentorNet, and has coached youth as well as inmates transitioning to the society on job hunting.

He is an adjunct faculty member at Prince George's Community College teaching project management. He has also provided dozens of workshops and training courses to hundreds of professionals in the areas of project management, engineering management, systems engineering, and strategy development. He is also founder of the Islamic Leadership Institute of America, a non-profit organization dedicated to the education and research of leadership and capacity building.

Ayman is inventor of several patents, publisher of dozens of articles and author, and has two Master degrees in Engineering Management & Systems Engineering; and Electrical Engineering from the University of Maryland and Cairo University respectively. He is a PMI certified project management professional (PMP), IBM certified IT Architect (ITA), Open Group Certified Master IT Architect (TOG), INCOSE Certified Systems Engineering Professional (CSEP), University of Maryland certified Systems Engineer and ASQ Certified Six Sigma Greenbelt (CSSGB). Ayman is also a member of PMI, INCOSE, IEEE, ASTD and ASQ. He has been an active contributor to the PMI Post Disaster Rebuild Methodology working group, and the INCOSE Information Systems Working Group.

Chapter 1

Introduction

Principles of Project Management

Unlike operations which follow standard operating procedures, a project is a unique endeavor which is supposed to be confined in duration. Projects are initiated to achieve objectives through the realization of deliverables. Throughout the project, artifacts will be created, such as project documents and reports. These artifacts will provide the project manager with guidance and control.

All projects are defined by the following unique characteristics,

1. Address a unique need.
2. Have a pre-defined start and end date, and hence are temporary.
3. Involve uncertainty and risk.
4. Evolve into greater levels of detail as progress on the project occurs.

The objective of a project is to realize a product or service deliverable. Job hunting is a complex endeavor that should be considered as a project. When you are looking for a job, you have specific goals and constraints in mind, such as a career objective, a salary, location, domain, industry, etc. Everyone's needs and interests in a job are unique and different from others. Additionally, you wish to make that move within a certain time frame and there are some elements of uncertainty in this job hunting process as you do not know who are potential employers, when will openings be available, who will respond to your application, and where will you eventually work. As you progress with your job hunt, you will delve into more details in the various areas of the job hunt. For example you will revise your resume a few times for improvements. You will research the industry and market in an iterative approach to get a better and more detailed understanding of the needs of employers and industry trends that drive these needs.

In the case of a job hunting project, your project deliverables are items that you wish to achieve and realize such as your resume, an interview meeting, a job offer and eventually a job. To realize these deliverables, some work has to be done and some artifacts such as project plans, control charts, and other project documents will be required.

Project Deliverables	Project Artifacts
End products of the job hunting project	Documents developed as part of your project work, used to assist you in realizing your deliverables
Resume Cover letter Interview Offer letter Employment agreement	Schedule To Do list Budget estimate Plans Risk assessment

Table 1 Definition and examples of project deliverables and artifacts.

So in summary, your job hunting process is a project with the following characteristics:

- Final deliverable and specifications: A job that meets career objectives, personal needs and obligations, and suits my specific environment.
- Start date: Today; End date: Define it to be according to your needs.
- Risk: Exist in many forms and sizes.
- Progression and iteration: Adjustable as more details are discovered.

The rest of the book will serve to illustrate how to apply the practices of project management to a job hunting project led by you. Assume that you are a software engineer and you recently lost your job as a result of the economic downturn, and you are seeking employment in the healthcare industry.

Chapter 2

Managing Your Job Hunting

Project Definition, Management Cornerstones, Elements of Project Success, Key Components of a Project Plan

وَمَا خَلَقْتُ الْجِنَّ وَالْإِنسَ إِلَّا لِيَعْبُدُونِ

Quran (51:56)

And I have not created the jinn (creation made out of fire) and men to any end other than that they may worship Me.

Meaning of Quranic parable 56, chapter 51 (Al-Thariyat)

Defining Your Project – Job Hunt Possible

At this point we agree that job hunting is a project. It has a specific purpose, timelines and hopefully is a temporary endeavor.

The next step is to write a statement of work (SOW) for your project, outlining the project objectives. It should be something similar to this:

> SOW: To secure a job as a software engineer within 3 months, with a comparable compensation and grade level to my most recent job.

Project Artifact 1 A job hunting project statement of work.

A statement of work is what a project sponsor provides the project manager to use as a starting point in initiating the project, describing the products or services to be offered by the project, and authorizing its initiation. In the case of a job hunting process, you can assign yourself the SOW, or have your spouse or close friend prepare one for you.

Cornerstones for Managing Your Job Hunt

Management comprises of four main cornerstones, which are easy to remember as **PO DC** (**P**ost **O**ffice in **DC**). These cornerstones are,

- Planning
- Organizing
- Directing
- Controlling

Similarly, to manage your job hunt, you will need to plan, organize, direct and control the process.

Planning the job hunt will involve forecasting potential alternatives to find a job, identifying forecasts and what-if scenarios that might occur, predicting possibilities and opportunities, as well as threats and risks. You might discover as an outcome of this process that you are not interested in working for an employer and instead will start a business or work as a contractor.

Planning involves defining mission and vision statements for your job hunt, and they both need to be connected to your mission and vision in life. Once these statements are clear, and you have done some initial planning, you can give yourself a charter to kick-off your job hunt project officially.

The project vision is what you expect your job to look like when you land it, and the project mission is the reason you want to work that job that you envision you will land. On the other hand, life vision and life mission apply to your entire life and includes your job vision and mission. Your charter is the authorization statement to actually start the project. It is the green light you give yourself after completing some initial thinking and planning to ensure that the project SOW is understood, valid and is what is really needed.

For our SOW above here are these project artifacts,

Vision (Project): To be working at a fortune 500 healthcare business as a software engineer.

Vision (Life): To contribute to the global well-being of patients and human healthcare through advanced software technologies.

Mission (Project): To solve problems related to healthcare services through developing and implementing sound software applications that enhance patient experience and the effectiveness of healthcare services.

Mission (Life): To be part of resolving the world's healthcare challenges through the utilization of software engineering.

Project Artifact 2 Project and life vision and mission statements.

Elements of Successful Job Hunting

Any project needs to meet three main criteria to be classified as a successful project. These are,

- Realize all deliverables needed
- Complete on or before due date
- Complete on or under budget

If one or more of these three criteria are not achieved, the project is considered unsuccessful and the degree of failure will depend on the magnitude and scope of the area of deficiency.

Similarly, your job hunting project needs to yield a job that meets your interests, experience, specifications and objectives – in other words meets your vision and mission. You also need to secure it within the time frame you have defined, and within the cost estimates you have calculated.

To ensure that your job hunting project is successful, you need to control and monitor your execution and the deliverables you are realizing. This means you need to assess the job openings you apply for, review the results of the application process, and track your schedule and the costs related.

Chapter 3

Job Hunting Life Cycle Phases

Concept, Design, Implementation, Testing, Deployment, Support, Disposal

كَيْفَ تَكْفُرُونَ بِاللَّهِ وَكُنتُمْ أَمْوَاتًا فَأَحْيَاكُمْ ثُمَّ يُمِيتُكُمْ ثُمَّ
يُحْيِيكُمْ ثُمَّ إِلَيْهِ تُرْجَعُونَ

Quran (2:28)

How can you refuse to acknowledge God, seeing that you were lifeless and He gave you life, and that He will cause you to die and then will bring you again to life, whereupon unto Him you will be brought back?

Meaning of Quranic parable 28, chapter 2 (The Cow)

Projects evolve over phases. They start with a concept phase and end with a disposal phase of the project deliverable. In between these two phases, various phases exist depending on the project's product.

In the case of a job hunting project, we start with an idea or concept. The concept phase is followed by some design work to develop plans, which leads to implementing steps in these plans, verifying our tests and deploying our job hunt. During the deployment phase we might need some support and follow-up on open issues. The project concludes by securing a job, closing all project activities, documenting lessons learned and the disposal of artifacts and deliverables that are no longer needed.

Figure 1 illustrates the job hunting project life cycle and process groups. For simplicity, process groups for only the concept and implementation phases are shown. Key milestones are shown along the project time axis. The vertical axis represents the amount of work conducted for each process group within a project phase. Also the figure illustrates the level of risk throughout the project. We notice that it decreases as more project work and planning get completed and that there could be a slight increase in risk at the time of deployment when you start interviews as new interactions and factors become relevant to the project. The accuracy of the cost and schedule estimates is lower at the beginning of the project, and increases as more planning occurs in the design phase.

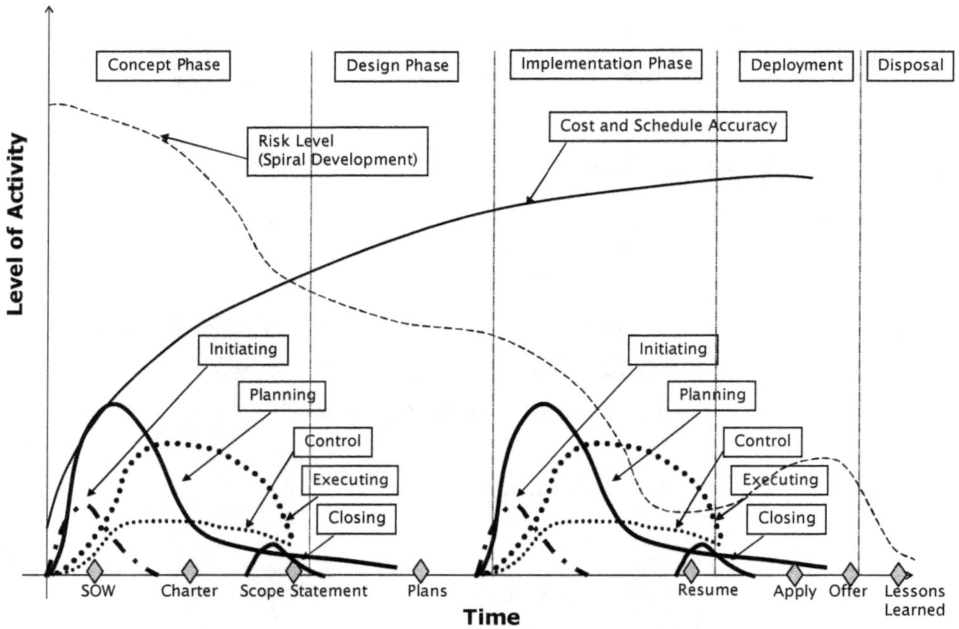

Figure 1 Job hunting project life cycle phases and process groups.

Concept

All projects including job hunting start with a concept phase. The concept phase is when you start to formulate ideas about getting a job. You come up with forecasts, scenarios, and alternatives. During the concept phase, you

also conduct research to identify trends and the feasibility of getting a job as defined in your charter.
It is important to allow yourself enough time to think through scenarios and possibilities to justify your job hunt. You might already be working and your interest is in finding a better opportunity, or you might be unemployed, or graduating from college and searching for a job to sustain your living expenses. Whatever the case might be, it is very important to utilize the concept phase effectively to ensure a solid foundation for your job hunting project. Other activities you would be doing during the concept phase are researching alternatives, validating your job vision and mission, and their alignment to your life-mission.

Examples of questions that would be analyzed during this phase are:

- Is it better to leave my current job and search for a new one?
- Should I seek an opportunity internally within my employer?
- Should I change industries, or stay in the same industry?
- Should I work as an employee, or should I be self-employed?
- What are my strengths and weaknesses?
- What opportunities and challenges exist in the marketplace?
- What tasks do I enjoy the most?
- What are my priorities and how are they organized?
- What is more important at the current time, compensation or experience?
- What are my dreams, and are they reflected in my vision?
- Does my mission take me to my dreams?
- What trends are taking place in the economy?

To come up with valid and solid answers to these questions, you need to understand your interests, abilities, strengths, and how to position them in reference to others seeking a job and in reference to the overall landscape.

An example of positioning oneself within an industry is a gentleman who attended one of my workshops; he was a professional photographer, working with law makers and high profile officials to cover events they attend. As budgets got cut, his job was eliminated. Instead of focusing on his still photography skills and decades of experience, he starting learning about digital video recording and editing. He realized that media is no longer just about hard copy newspapers, but also about online news outlets which require still pictures, video clips, and other multimedia.

Some signs to help you identify trends in the economy are reports on jobless claims, durable goods, home sales, consumer confidence, retail sales and lending patterns. To learn about opportunities and challenges in the marketplace, you should follow press releases, network with professional associations, attend conferences, subscribe to trade publications and website, and receive email updates from professional blogs.

The concept phase starts with initiation processes that launch the project concept. These processes define the scope of the concept phase, and initial planning. A group of planning processes implemented in the concept phase allows us to define plans and guidelines to control our project during this phase. Control processes are needed to control, track, and monitor progress and changes during the concept phase. The concept phase will end with closing processes that assure us that we have completed the concept phase and are now ready to move into designing our job hunt.

These process groups repeat for each phase of the project – concept, design, implementation, testing, deployment and disposal - and are iterative and progressive.

For the concept phase, the key processes in each of these process groups and their deliverables are listed in Table 2. Your project will contain project artifacts which are interim deliverables that will assist you in becoming organized and enhance your vision and guidance. These artifacts will ensure you achieve your project deliverables in accordance to your project plans. An example of an artifact is the project charter. It is not part of the final product deliverable – unlike the resume or cover letter.

Process Group	Process Name	Project Artifacts	Project Deliverable
Initiation Processes	Develop job hunt charter	Job hunting charter	
Planning Processes	Develop job hunt scope management plan Define job hunt scope statement	Job hunting scope management plan Job hunting project scope statement	Job scope statement
Execution Processes	Direct and manage the job hunt	Action items Job hunting project work performance status	
Control Processes	Control changes to the job hunt Control job hunt scope	Change requests Baselined scope	
Closing Processes	Close job hunt concept phase	Completed concept phase closure checklist	

Table 2 Key project management processes' artifacts and job hunting deliverables during the concept phase

Remember that project artifacts are items that are not of interest to the project sponsor, but rather to the project manager. You are wearing the hats of both the sponsor and project manager and need to be aware of the difference between both roles and the value each brings to your job hunting project. Artifacts are project process outputs used for achieving and delivering the project's deliverables. The project deliverables are the items that you are interested in realizing, such as a completed and ready-to-use resume, an interview invitation, an offer letter, or a job agreement.

It is important to note that there are many other processes in each of the process groups above. However, the ones mentioned above are the most important for this phase. Examples of other processes are communications management planning, risk management planning, cost management planning, and many other processes.

The concept phase starts with developing the project charter. An example for your job hunt is illustrated in Project Artifact 3.

Charter: Secure a job in the healthcare industry in the area of software engineering within 3 months, with a cost of no more than $2000; to realize a comparable or better compensation package than my current compensation, and hold a responsibility equivalent to or higher than my current responsibilities.

Project Artifact 3 Sample job hunting project charter.

Some planning occurs during the concept phase, which is mostly related to developing a plan to manage the job hunting project scope.

Planning accounts for the highest percentage of time on any project. Hence, it is important to give yourself enough time to plan your job hunting concept. Do not rush into designing your resume and applying to job openings without first giving yourself enough time to plan the job hunt concept. The job hunt planning that occurs during the concept phase will enable you to identify the boundaries of your job search, so you will not waste time and resources in applying to openings that might not be of high interest or do not match your criteria. Moreover, planning during this phase ensures that the rest of your project activities are all aligned towards the correct goals and objectives, and more importantly, that you are pursuing the correct job type for your strengths, weaknesses and interests given the surrounding conditions and factors. As mentioned earlier, common job types are part-time employment, full-time employments, self-employment, franchising, contracting, business owner, freelancer, or any combination of these.

The planning process will yield a scope management plan which provides guidance on how to create, change, verify and control the job hunt scope. An example of the project scope management plan is outlined in Project Artifact 4. The scope management plan is a very important artifact, even on small projects. It ensures that the project does not go off-target and avoid scope creep, by adding or reducing the final product deliverable.

Project Scope Management Plan

This scope management plan comprises of the following sections:

A. Definition of a scope statement

The job hunting scope statement will define the project objectives such as the target deadline for finding a new job, the cost estimated allocated to the job hunting process, and other key features of the job of interest.

B. Process to develop the scope statement

On this job hunting project, I will brainstorm, research the market, interview others and study trends to develop a clear, realistic and achievable project scope. All brainstormed thoughts and ideas will be documented and enumerated for ease of reference and elaboration.

C. Methods to verify project scope

On a weekly basis I will compare actual work I conduct on my job hunting project to the project scope statement and other project management tools to ensure that I am within the scope of the project and the features of the job.

D. Methods to control project scope

I will use work status reports, progress reports, work breakdown structure and activity lists, along with cost and schedule variances to control scope. The scope statement will be baselined once defined. Changes to the scope will require that I conduct an analysis of the impact of change to the project, and also the approval of others that I designate as members of the change control board.

Project Artifact 4 Sample job hunting project scope management plan

A key output of the concept phase is a clear job hunt project scope statement defining your interest in hunting for a job. The scope statement could be as small as a few paragraphs or as big as a small document of several pages. The scope statement will comprise of various elements the most important are; a clear definition of the objectives of the project, a product description – the job, constraints impacting the project, acceptance criteria for the final product and key milestones.

Notice that there is another scope statement known as the job scope statement, as illustrated in Table 2. The job scope statement is included in the project scope statement and is used to define the job itself. Since the job is what interests you the most, we consider the job scope statement to be one of the project deliverables, whereas the job hunt project scope statement is a project artifact.

Job Hunting Scope Statement

Objective

Secure a job in the healthcare industry in the area of software engineering within 3 months, as an independent consultant, with a cost of no more than $2000. Realize a total compensation package which is 25% higher than my current compensation, and hold a technical and leadership responsibilities higher than my current responsibilities.

Product

Offer clinical application consulting services to hospitals and physician offices in the areas of clinical care, care planning, patient diagnostics, prescription management services, and data retrieval. Focus on specialized pediatric hospitals, pediatric physicians, specialists, and dentists. Specialize in telemedicine, hand-held and desktop access, and interfaces to backend enterprise systems for billing and scheduling.

Constraints

Areas of interest are Washington DC, Chicago, Houston, San Diego metro areas.

Criteria for selecting a job

Compensation, location, medical provider type, application type, leadership responsibility.

Milestones

Resume, Network List, Tracking Tools, Applying, Interviews, Offers, Lessons Learned.

Project Artifact 5 Sample job hunting scope statement.

The main execution process during the concept phase is to manage and control the concept phase. This will give you the assurance that you are progressing on your project and achieving work towards the job scope statement. Progress can be tracked using a status report that you develop for yourself to document accomplishments and next steps. You should develop a spreadsheet to capture action items, a to do list, which will include fields for the date the action item was identified, the description of the action item, its priority, status, closure date, and domain.

Control processes are required to ensure that you do not change the scope of the project while you are still in the concept phase. Control also ensures that you are spending project expenses wisely and working at a reasonable rate. During the concept phase, you should not be spending much more other on activities to assist you in defining your job scope, and job hunt project scope statements. Examples of such activities that might incur expenses are research costs, access to databases, reports, trade journal subscriptions, attending industry workshops, or joining a professional organization. It is important to note that since we have not entered the design phase of the job hunt, we don't have complete plans for the whole project yet, and as a result, we are blind to all the resources needed on the project. Hence, it is important to use good judgment about how much to invest for research and concept phases activities.

Control can be achieved through the use of charts and logs to record changes. To identify a change, a baseline needs to be achieved and any changes compared to the baseline. Hence, once the scope statement is defined, it should be documented and baselined. If a change needs to occur to it, you should follow the process you defined in your scope control section of your scope management plan. You might want to create a change control board that assists you in making scope change decisions. Depending on your situation the members of such a board could be your spouse, parent, professional coach, instructor, a close friend in the field, a team member, or one of your references. You will seek approval from these individuals in the form of advice by explaining the original scope and your planned changes. Depending on the responses you receive, you can make a sound decision on whether to change the scope or not after, of course, assessing all impacts.

You can conclude the concept phase by completing a checklist that provides you with the assurance that the main areas of work have been accomplished and completed. A sample checklist for the concept phase is illustrated in Project Artifact 6.

Job Hunting Concept Phase Checklist		
Job scope defined	Yes	No
Job hunting project scope defined	Yes	No
Scope management plan documented	Yes	No
Scope statement baselined	Yes	No
Action items captured	Yes	No
Performance documented	Yes	No

Project Artifact 6 Sample job hunting concept phase checklist.

Table 3 illustrates key inputs, outputs, tools and techniques for the job hunting concept phase, along with sample embodiments.

	Artifact	Realized Project Artifact
Inputs	Job objectives Career vision Career mission Economic factors Industry trends Current employment / job status SOW	Objective list Vision statement Mission statement List of economic factors and their impact levels List of key trends Employment trends and demands Statement of Work
Outputs	Charter Scope statement	Project charter documented in word Scope statement documented in word
Tools	Ideation tools Flow charts Spreadsheets Trend reports Internet search engines Job websites Social networking	MindMapper Visio, Power Point, Pencil and Paper Excel Word Google News, Yahoo Business, Newspapers Yahoo Hot Jobs, Professional Associations Linkedin, FaceBook, Twitter, Delicious, Digg
Techniques	Brainstorming Analysis Forecasting Interviews Networking	Statements Cost charts Control charts Communications

Table 3 Inputs, outputs, tools and techniques for the concept phase of a job hunting project.

Design

The design phase focuses on designing your job hunting campaign. It outlines the approaches and plans you will pursue. It defines plans to guide your job hunting and manage scope, cost, schedule, risk, communications and other key areas of your project. These plans are like maps to help you stay focused and aligned to your mission.

Several important plans that are needed to guide your job hunting project are:

- Time utilization management planning
- Cost management planning
- Risk management planning
- Communications management planning
- Team management planning
- Quality management planning

These planning activities will be discussed at length in the next few chapters. However it is important to note that detailed planning or the designing of you job hunt project will start with the scope statement and end with a bunch of documents that explain to you how to do things on the project; things like managing risk, controlling costs, tracking schedule and accomplishments, staying in touch with others, and more.

Table 4 summarizes the key processes during the design phase for each process group used during this phase.

Process Group	Process Name	Project Artifacts	Project Deliverable
Initiation Processes	Develop phase objectives	Design phase objectives Scope of work during design phase	Target industries and roles defined
Planning Processes	Develop time utilization management plans Develop cost management plans Develop risk management plans Develop communications management plans Develop team management plans Develop quality management plans	Job hunting schedule management plan Job hunting cost management plan Job hunting risk management plan Job hunting communications management plan Job hunting team / stakeholder management plan Job hunting quality management plan	Target hire date Job acceptance criteria
Execution Processes	Direct and manage the job hunt	Job hunting schedule Job hunting cost estimates Job hunting expense logs Job hunting communications log Contact list Action items Job hunting project work performance status	Canned email responses templates Resume template Cover letter template
Control Processes	Control changes to the job hunt Control job hunt scope	Change requests Baselined scope	
Closing Processes	Close job hunt design phase	Completed design phase closure checklist	

Table 4 Key project management processes' artifacts and job hunting deliverables during the design phase

Table 5 summarizes the most important inputs, outputs, tools and techniques during the design phase.

	Project Artifact or Resource	Realization of Artifact or Resource
Inputs	Scope statement Economic factors Industry trends Current employment / job status	Scope statement documented in word
Outputs	Cost management plan Schedule management plan Scope management plan Communications management plan Team management plan Quality management plan	Maps in the form of job hunting project plans to guide you on your job hunting project
Tools	Work breakdown structure Databases and repositories Internet Templates Lists Interviews	Hierarchical structured lists and tables to organize action items, to do activities and other important project information
Techniques	Analysis Forecasting Decision-making Information retrieval Estimation Cause-effect Prioritization Expert judgment Decomposition Flow charting	Documented reports with ranked alternatives and defined criteria

Table 5 Main inputs, outputs, tools and technique for job hunting campaign design phase.

Implementation Phase

The implementation phase is when the bulk of the work gets done in accordance to the plans developed in the design phase. It is important to note that although these phases are sequential, some implementation work gets done in other phases as part of the executing processes of the project phase. Remember that the presence of the initiating, planning, control, executing and closing processes in all phases results in an iterative and progressive project. The bulk of execution work gets done in the implementation phase; however, some execution also occurs in other phases to lesser degrees, as illustrated in Figure 2 below. This should not be confused with the fact that moving from one phase to another is mostly about reaching milestones, which are usually the outputs of that phase.

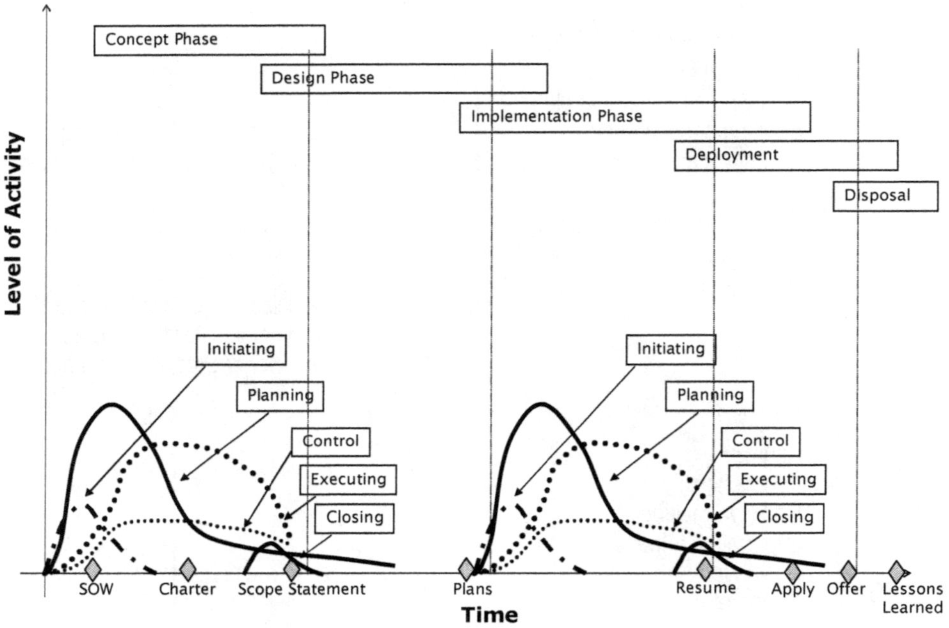

Figure 2 Job hunting project phases and key milestones.

The main processes that take place during implementation are executing processes, such as:

- Managing and directing the job hunt execution
- Work performance information collection
- Establishing relationships and networking
- Information distribution
- Performing technical activities to realize project deliverables

These processes will be discussed at length in future chapters. Other processes that will also occur during the implementation phase from other process groups are:

Initiating:

- Scope definition for implementation

Planning updates:

- Risk planning
- Risk identification
- Risk response planning
- Risk qualification and quantification

Control:

- Cost control
- Schedule control
- Risk control
- Stakeholder control

Closing:

- Accepting project deliverables

The main inputs, outputs, tools and techniques using during the implementation phase are summarized in Table 7.

	Project Artifact or Resource	Realization of Artifact or Resource
Inputs	Cost management plan Schedule management plan Scope management plan Communications management plan Team management plan Quality management plan	Scope statement documented in word
Outputs	Project deliverables Control reports Progress reports	Resumes Bios Network lists Target employers Portfolios and accomplishments Cover letters Accessories Available budgets Promotional tools Search tools Interview needs Registered events Responses Tip sheets Memberships in associations or networks Awards Certifications Publications Developed skills Demonstrated experiences Recommendations and endorsements Cost, schedule, risk variance reports Updated plans Updated risk logs Cash flow statements Progress and status reports
Tools	Work breakdown structure Databases and repositories Internet Templates Lists	Custom developed tools Web-based tools Issue lists Dependency lists Risk registers Conference calls

	Project Artifact or Resource	Realization of Artifact or Resource
Techniques	Documentation Presentation Communication Negotiation Meetings Reading Studying Learning Critical thinking	Word processors Spreadsheets Presentations Books Blogs Face-face meetings Professional events, conferences Training, workshops Updated plans

Table 6 Main inputs, outputs, tools and technique for job hunting implementation phase.

Deployment Phase

The deployment phase is when you actually go out and start applying for positions and interviewing. The deployment phases uses the guidance in the plans you have already developed during the design phase, along with the project deliverables accepted in the implementation phase to deploy your talent and capabilities in the market place.

Again, realize that during deployment, you could be updating plans, implementing a few things here and there, like new versions of your resume. The reverse also applies that during the implementation phase, it is possible that you apply for a position even though you don't have all project deliverables ready and accepted. However, the bulk of your deployment work should occur in the deployment phase after you have achieved deployment milestones, which is indicated by "resume" on Figure 2.

The main processes that take place during deployment are executing processes and are almost the same as implementation. They are listed below and will be discussed further in later chapters in the book.

- Managing and directing the job hunt execution
- Work performance information collection
- Establishing, updating and maintaining relationships and networking
- Information distribution
- Leverage stakeholder relationships

Other processes that will also occur during the implementation phase from other process groups are:

Initiating:

- Scope definition for deployment

Planning updates:

- Risk planning
- Risk identification
- Risk response planning
- Risk qualification and quantification

Control:

- Cost control
- Schedule control
- Risk control
- Stakeholder control

Closing:

- Realizing deployment deliverables
- Realizing project objectives and goals

The main inputs, outputs, tools and techniques using during the deployment phase are summarized in Table 7.

	Project Artifact or Resource	Realization of Artifact or Resource
Inputs	Project deliverables Project artifacts	Resumes Biographies Network lists Target employers Portfolios and accomplishments Cover letters Accessories Available budgets Promotional tools Search tools Interview needs Registered events Responses Tip sheets Memberships in associations

	Project Artifact or Resource	Realization of Artifact or Resource
		Awards Certifications Publications Developed skills Demonstrated experiences Recommendations and endorsements Cost, schedule, risk variance reports Updated plans Updated risk logs Cash flow statements Progress and status reports
Outputs	Final project deliverables Project objectives and goals	Application responses Interview invitations Interviews Offer letters Employment agreements Contracts
Tools	Work breakdown structure Databases and repositories Lists Reports	Custom developed tools Web-based tools Issue lists Dependency lists Follow up lists Risk registers Conf calls
Techniques	Presentation Communication Negotiation Meetings	Video, audio, slide presentations Publications, blogs Face-face meetings Conf calls, IM, networking tools Attending events, conferences, workshops Updated plans

Table 7 Main inputs, outputs, tools and technique for job hunting deployment phase.

Disposal Phase

The disposal phase is the final phase of the project. It starts after you have achieved the objectives of your job hunt and secured an employment contract, or some agreement for contract work. The disposal phase involves some initiation processes, planning, execution, control and closing just like any other phase. However, it mostly focuses on closing.

The disposal phase will ensure that all project artifacts are completed, reviewed, and checked for archival. Lessons learned will be documented throughout the project, but also mostly during this phase. Lessons learned are important for sustainability and growth on future similar projects. When documenting lessons learned, you will document experiences that you witnessed and the expected outcomes for these experiences. Experiences could be positive or negative, but the outcomes are usually unexpected. You then plan and think about what the expected outcomes would have been and how to bridge the gaps if they were negative outcomes, or ensure repeatability if they are positive experiences.

The main processes that take place during disposal are closing processes. They are listed below and will be discussed further in later chapters in the book.

- Closing open activities and items
- Documenting lessons learned
- Establishing, updating and maintaining relationships and networking

Other processes that will also occur during the implementation phase from other process groups are:

Initiating:

- Scope definition for disposal

Closing:

- Realizing project deliverables
- Realizing project objectives and goals

The main inputs, outputs, tools and techniques using during the disposal phase are summarized in Table 8.

	Project Artifact or Resource	Realization of Artifact or Resource
Inputs	Final project deliverables Realized project objectives	Application responses Interview invitations Interviews Offer letters Employment agreements Contracts
Outputs	Lessons learned Closed issues Baselined project deliverables	Lessons learned spreadsheet Baselined compensation package Contacts and networks
Tools	Lessons learned templates Lists	Spreadsheets, word processors Social network tools Follow up lists
Techniques	Lessons learned analysis Issue management	

Table 8 Main inputs, outputs, tools and technique for job hunting disposal phase.

Job Hunting Management Processes

Chapter 4

Initiation, Planning, Execution, Controlling, Closing

وَلَا تَقُولَنَّ لِشَيْءٍ إِنِّي فَاعِلٌ ذَٰلِكَ غَدًا إِلَّا أَن يَشَاءَ اللَّهُ

Quran (18:23-24)

And never say about anything, "Behold, I shall do this tomorrow," without (adding), "if God so wills."

Meaning of Quranic parable 23-24, chapter 18 (Al-Kahf)

Initiating the Job Hunt

Initiation occurs throughout the beginning of all phases of the job hunt process. However, the largest amount of initiation processes work occurs in the concept phase. Initiation mostly involves scoping the project and the various phases. During the concept phase, initiation will address the overall project charter and scope. During each of the other phases, initiation will address any scope updates to that particular phase. The interest and focus of initiation processes will differ across the different phases as summarized below in Table 9.

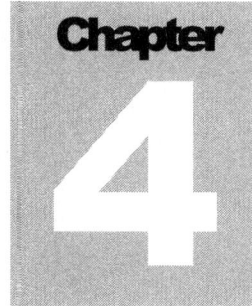

	Focus	Objective	Examples
Concept	Define and develop the project charter. Defining the scope for the entire project.	Clear understanding of all dimensions of the project. Reasonable understanding of risk elements and complexity level.	High level estimate for total duration, cost, and main deliverables. Charter statement.
Design	Refining the scope for the design.	How many plans are needed The level of depth and detail of each plan. How to best customize methodologies and approaches to the project.	The names of project plans to be developed. The depth of the cost management plan. How to customize the approach in this book to the project.
Implementation	Refining the scope of implementation tools and approaches.	Understand how many implementation approaches will be used. Knowing to what extent approaches will be used and the percent of time and cost for each approach.	Thresholds for considering a resume ready. How many resumes to have on hand at any time. How many social networks to utilize.
Deployment	Refining the scope of deployment activities	Understand volume and performance expectations for various deployment activities. Define thresholds to determine cost and schedule control.	Number of interviews should we strive for on a day. Expenses for a particular activity.
Disposal	Defining scope of closing activities	Identify the level of detail of the lessons learned. Identify the percent of issues that are closed to consider acceptable to close the project.	Number of lessons learned captured. Significance levels of outcomes experienced.

Table 9 Initiation processes across the various project phases.

Planning the Job Hunt

Planning occurs throughout the project during all phases of the job hunt, and it will have a different focus in each phase as summarized below in Table 10. However the most intensive planning will usually occur during the design phase. Planning continues throughout the project and is mostly to reflect updates to situations and account for risks and other factors that might impact original plans. Additionally, as the project progresses, more details will be uncovered and plans will become more detailed.

The main planning processes are:

- Job hunting scope planning
- Job hunting work planning
- Job hunt activity planning
- Job hunting resource planning
- Job hunting schedule planning
- Job hunting cost estimating and budgeting
- Planning your job hunting team
- Job hunting communications planning
- Job hunting quality planning
- Purchasing and contracting planning for the job hunt

	Focus	Objective	Examples
Concept	Plan for the control of scope and develop quick and simple plans to be able to understand the strategic objectives of the job hunt	Quickly and easily have a good idea of the project deliverables and objectives, as well as the project constraints, risks, schedule and cost.	The scope management plan which describes how to define scope, control and verify scope.
Design	Detailed planning for the full job hunt	Detailing cost estimates, schedule, milestone dates, risks, approaches for communicating, leveraging stakeholders and detailing plans for executing, controlling and closing activities	A communications plan which discusses how to contact recruiters among other communication details.
Implementation	Updates and refinements to plans as new details are identified and/or progress changes	Ensuring that plans are current and versatile	Updates to the risk response plan as more details about risks unfold
Deployment	Updates and refinements to plans as new details are identified and/or progress changes	Ensuring that plans are current and versatile	Updates to the communications management plan to reflect the usage of twitter as a communication tool

	Focus	Objective	Examples
Disposal	Short term plans to close the project or refinements and updates	Ensuring the plans are current and versatile	Updates to the lessons learned plan

Table 10 Planning processes' focus and objectives across the various project phases.

Executing the Job Hunt

Throughout the job hunting project, you will be executing processes and activities to accomplish work. The majority of execution occurs during the implementation phase However, all other phases have execution activities occurring. For example, during the concept phase, some management to the brainstorming and strategic thinking has to occur, some work will need to get implemented, even if it as simple as running to the stationary store to purchase paper and pencils to use in your brainstorming sessions. Table 11 summarizes the focus of the execution processes across the different project phases. Key execution processes during the project are:

- Developing job hunting deliverables
- Establish connections and network
- Distribute information
- Develop self

	Focus	Objective	Examples
Concept	Developing high level job hunting deliverables	Have clear focus of job of interest	Job scope statement. Career objective.
Design	Research and collect information to best develop plans that allow for optimum positioning	Position the job of interest in the context of project constraints and environmental factors	Collect information on travel and conference fees to assist in budget planning
Implementation	Identifying templates for job hunting deliverables for distribution readiness during deployment. Develop self in all areas. Collecting information to	Efficient, modular and updated information distribution. Increase technical competitiveness in marketplace.	Developing the resume template. Developing a portfolio. Developing the resume.

	Focus	Objective	Examples
	utilize during deployment for job hunt.	Uniquely position self.	Attending specialized workshops.
Deployment	Producing the final delivery of the job hunting project.	Realize the final deliverables.	Send resumes to hiring managers. Attend networking events. Develop consulting proposals. Attend interviews. Review offers. Negotiate offers.
Disposal	Documenting lessons learned. Finishing work that is open.	Archive and store valuable information. Dispose of drafts and working documents. Communicate appreciation to stakeholders.	Going through check-lists to ensure thank you notes were sent. Document lesson learned and place in project folder.

Table 11 Execution processes' focus and objectives across the various project phases.

Controlling the Job Hunt

Control is an essential element to the success of projects. The majority of projects fail, and in some industries, the rate of failure is much higher than others. Failure is usually due to one of two main reasons; either poor planning or poor control. Poor execution can lead to failed projects as well; however, the root causes of failure usually come from planning and are exuberated through ineffective controls.

Effective project controls should occur throughout the full life cycle of your job hunting project. You need to make sure that you don't go off tangent during any phase. During the early days of the project, you need to ensure that you are within the reasonable timeframes and costs that your statement of work outlines. You might not even know what these values are and hence they might not be part of the statement of work, which makes staying focused more challenged. A good balance is needed during the concept phase to ensure that you still have given yourself enough chance to explore all potential interests, and at the same time complete the concept phase before you are in a sensitive position.

The main control processes across the different project phases are listed below, and the focus and objective during each phase are summarized below in .

	Focus	Objective	Examples
Concept	Control scope Control cost Control schedule	Ensure concept phase does not take longer than needed and does not expand into unrealistic areas that can not be realized	A daily progress report to track amount of scope defined.
Design	Control scope Control cost Control schedule	Ensure design work is within scope and avoid scope creep. Maintain cost and schedule.	Weekly cost and schedule variance reports. Weekly scope verification.
Implementation	Control scope Control cost Control schedule Control delivery and performance Control deliverable quality Control risk	Ensure implementation work is within scope and avoid scope creep. Maintain cost and schedule. Ensure deliverables meet expectations. Ensure progress is as expected. Ensure risk is addressed.	Weekly cost and schedule variance. Weekly work complete reports. Weekly risk status reports. Deliverable quality control reports.
Deployment	Control scope Control cost Control schedule Control delivery and performance Control stakeholders Control risk	Ensure deployment work is within scope and avoid scope creep. Maintain cost and schedule. Ensure deliverables meet expectations. Ensure progress is as expected. Ensure risk is addressed.	Weekly cost and schedule variance. Weekly work complete reports. Weekly risk status reports. Deliverable quality control reports. Weekly project objectives status report.
Disposal	Control stakeholders	Ensure expectations are met.	All open correspondence is closed.

Table 12 Control processes' focus and objectives across the various project phases.

Job hunt scope verification and control

- Job hunt cost control
- Job hunt schedule control
- Job hunt deliverables quality control

- Controlling expectations of job hunt stakeholders
- Job hunt risk control
- Controlling job hunt project execution and delivery
- Integrated job hunt change control

Closing the Job Hunt

The closing processes occur at the end of each phase and the end of the project. You may decide to close your project for any of the following reasons,

- Project objectives achieved
- Project objectives drastically changed
- Project failed to accomplish its deliverables as planned
- Changes in life mission and vision

The main processes related to closing the project are,

- Terminating agreements or contracts
- Closure procedure

These two processes focus on ending any outstanding agreements you might have for your job hunting; for example, it may be a web hosting agreement where you post your resume, an account with a social network, or an agreement with a head hunter. The second process focuses on implementing steps to put the project immediately on hold. Examples include stopping all expenses, retuning remaining funds to source accounts, starting the lessons learned documentation, and archiving any needed files. Table 13 summarizes the focus and objectives of closing processes in each phase of the job hunting project.

	Focus	Objective	Examples
Concept	End the concept phase	Ensure that criteria to move to the design have been achieved. Learn from experiences during concept phase.	Job hunting charter is developed and complete. Actual time spent compared to expected time spent and information used for better planning during

	Focus	Objective	Examples
			the design and implementation phases.
Design	End the design phase	Ensure criteria are achieved. Learn from experiences.	Document lessons learned during concept phase. Job hunting schedule is complete and baselined.
Implementation	End the implementation phase	Ensure criteria are achieved. Learn from experiences.	Resume, presentation and portfolio are ready for deployment.
Deployment	End the deployment phase	Ensure criteria are achieved. Learn from experiences.	Interviews have been conducted, offers received and meeting held as planned.
Disposal	End the project	Ensure project objectives are achieved. Learn from experiences. Settle agreements and contracts.	Make outstanding payments to any vendors. Close financial sheets. Return any resources borrowed.

Table 13 Closing processes' focus and objectives across the various project phases.

Chapter 5

The Scope of the Job Hunt

Scope Definition, Work, Scope Verification, Scope Control

وَآتَاكُم مِّن كُلِّ مَا سَأَلْتُمُوهُ وَإِن تَعُدُّواْ نِعْمَتَ اللّهِ لاَ تُحْصُوهَا إِنَّ الإِنسَانَ لَظَلُومٌ كَفَّارٌ

Quran (14:34)

And [always] does He give you something out of what you may be asking of Him; and should you try to count God's blessings, you could never compute them. [And yet,] behold, man is indeed most persistent in wrongdoing, stubbornly ingrate!

Meaning of Quranic parable 34, chapter 14 (Ibrahim)

Unlike the blessings of our Creator, which are countless and boundless, your job hunting project should have a limited scope, and will mostly be defined during the concept phase and the early part of the design phase. The scope management planning set of processes mentioned earlier in chapter three, as part of the design phase, comprises of defining the job hunt scope, defining the work to be completed for the job hunt, how to verify the scope, and how to control the scope.

Job Hunt Scope

The processes involved in defining scope start with developing the charter and then a draft scope statement during the concept phase.

During the early part of the design phase, the draft scope statement will be refined and finalized. Refer to Project Artifact 5 for a sample scope statement for your job hunting.

Some questions to ask during the scope development process in the design phase are,

- How much can I afford to invest in finding a new job?
- Do I want to work as an employee, self-employed, contractor, business owner, or some hybrid of all?
- How much is the minimum acceptable compensation?
- How soon do I need a job?
- How much time can I sustain without a job?
- What are the thresholds at which I must start changing minimum acceptable compensation?
- What objectives do I strive to achieve in my job?
- What are my geographical area constraints?
- What times of day / night am I willing to work?
- What kind of healthcare organization do I want to work for?
- What kind of applications or products do I want to be involved with on a daily basis in my job in the healthcare industry?
- What kind of end users do I wish to serve?
- What kind of career goals do I strive for in my next job?
- What are the relative priorities of my career goals?
- What personal constraints impact my job hunting plans?
- What are some of the major milestones I should recognize on my project?

In critiquing your scope, you can ask yourself questions like these,

- How SMART (Specific, Measurable, Attainable, Relevant and Timely) are my job hunting objectives?
- Is my scope specific and concise? Am I clear what position type, level, industry, product and user I want to be involved with?

- Can I measure my scope statement? Can I determine if the position is exceptional, expected, average, worse that my aspirations?
- Can I achieve the scope I am striving for? Do I have the experience, skills, motivation, knowledge, network, abilities and environment to support realizing the scope?
- Is the scope relevant to my career and life mission and vision?
- Can I achieve the scope within the timeframe defined? How rigid are these timeframes?
- Is my scope risky? How many elements of unknowns exist in my scope statement? How complex is my scope statement?
- Have I critically thought about my scope statement? Are there other alternatives to my scope statement? How many other variations of the scope statement can I come up with?

Work Needed

Once your job hunting project scope is documented, you need to baseline it. This means that you will not allow yourself to make any changes to it without going through some process of checks and balances. We will take more about this control process in a few sections of this chapter.

The next step is to decompose the baselined scope statement into several major areas of work. We then subsequently break down each of these areas of work into more detailed areas of work and so on, until we reach a level of detail that is small enough to control and manage. Usually, the lowest level of work is one that can be completed in a block of 4 hours for this type of project.

Project Artifact 7 below illustrated a partial job hunting project work breakdown structure (WBS); consider the WBS to be a large hierarchical To Do list. There is no one-size-fits-all WBS; your WBS will be different from other people, and might even change during the course of your job hunting project. The main attributes of the WBS is that is decomposes your scope statement into areas of work that you need to accomplish to realize the final project deliverables – your dream job. Notice that each work item is uniquely enumerated and identified. The identification of each work item will allow you to easily track work completed later on the project in addition to mapping it future issues identified, risks, costs or other project related information.

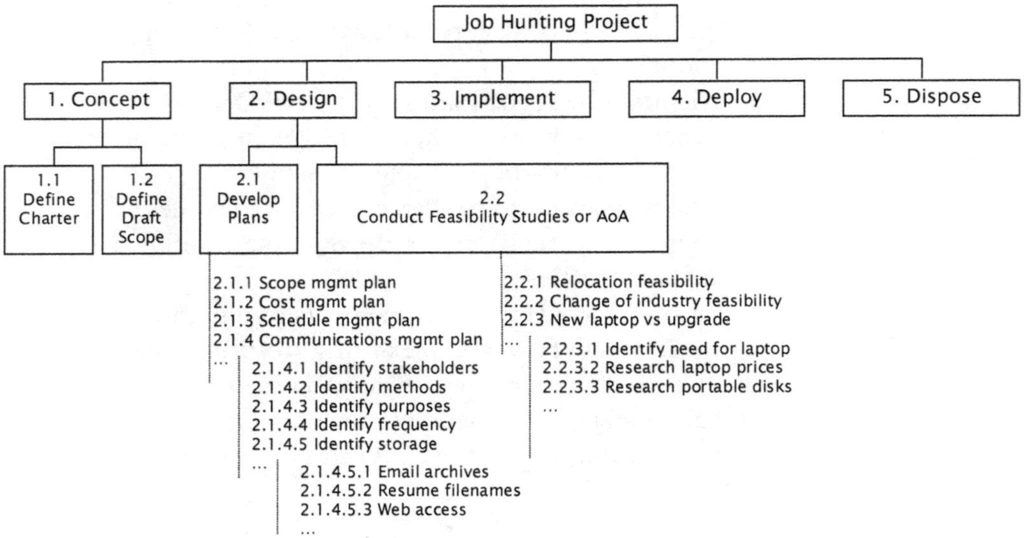

Project Artifact 7 Partial work breakdown structure for job hunting project based on job hunting process.

Your job hunting project work can be broken down based on processes or steps to be completed on the project as indicated in Project Artifact 7. However, this is not the only way; you might decide that you prefer to break down your work based on final project deliverables as illustrated in Project Artifact 8. In this case, instead of describing processes that need to be completed, you describe products that need to be realized.

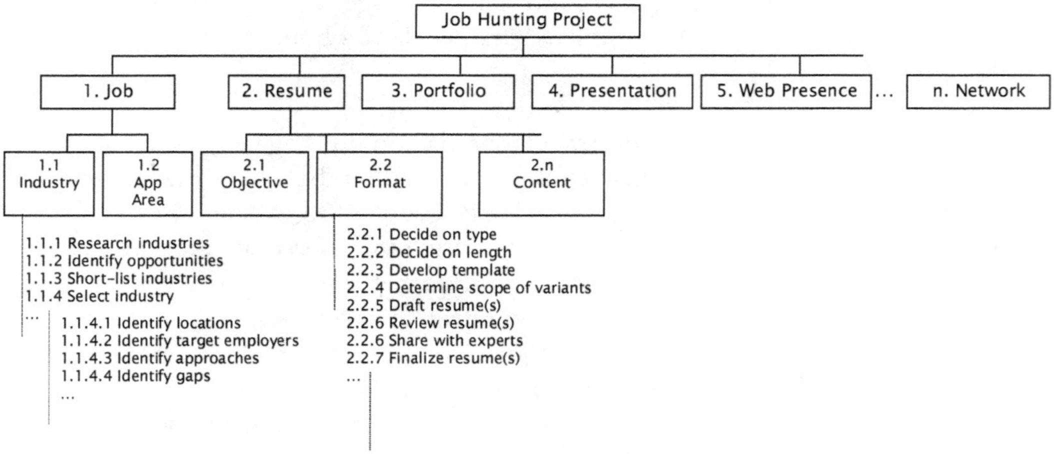

Project Artifact 8 Partial work breakdown structure for job hunting based on final product.

Are We Focused?

As part of scope management, is important to ensure that you are always within the scope of your job hunting project. This will ensure that you stayed focused and do not fall into the trick of scope creep. The best approach to detect scope creep is to verify that the activity you are working on can trace back to a work item in the WBS.

Activities are discussed later in the book. However, for clarification, an activity is a work item assigned a time slot and resources. If an activity can not be tracked back to a work item in the WBS, then most probably either your WBS is not detailed enough, or the activity is out of scope.

Enforcing the Focus

If you detect out of scope activities, determine their importance and urgency. Based on the findings, be determined to either change your scope or cancel the activity. A log that can be used to keep track of out of scope activities is shown below in Project Artifact 9.

Out of Scope ID	Activity Name	Description	Importance Level (1 - 5)	Urgency Level	Date Detected	Impact	Decision
1	Purchase premium resume paper	Go to shopping center to order 100 sheets of high quality colored resume paper	2	1	6/1/2008	Cost: High Schedule: Med.	Drop
2	Spell proof resume	Review resume 3 times using 3 different approaches to check for any typos	5	4	5/17/2008	Cost: V. Low Schedule: Med.	Update WBS
3	Applied to software engineer at CIO office	Applied to CIO at a shipping company for software engineer	2	4	4/3/2008	Cost: Med. Schedule: High	Drop

Project Artifact 9 Sample job hunting scope creep log.

Chapter

6

Job Hunt Time Utilization

Activity Definition, Activity Sequencing, Activity Resource Estimating, Activity Duration Estimation, Schedule Development, Schedule Control

وَيَوْمَ يَحْشُرُهُمْ كَأَن لَّمْ يَلْبَثُواْ إِلاَّ سَاعَةً مِّنَ النَّهَارِ يَتَعَارَفُونَ

بَيْنَهُمْ

Quran (10:45)

And on the Day when He shall gather them [unto Himself, it will seem to them] as if they had not tarried [on earth] longer than an hour of a day, knowing one another.

Meaning of Quranic parable 45, chapter 10 (Younis)

Getting Active

In order to execute work on the project, you need to transform your WBS work items into activities. Activities are work items with defined resources and defined start and end times or dates. Activities also require that work items be sequenced; hence, dependencies among work items will need to be identified. An activity list requires the ability to answer the following questions.

- What needs to be done to accomplish the work item?
- What steps are needed and what is the sequence of these steps for each work item?
- How long does each step require?
- Are steps dependent on other steps?
- Are activities dependent on other activities?

- What is the dependency like? Do I need to finish one activity to start the other? Could the two activities start together? Can I start one in order to finish another?
- How can I estimate the time for each activity?

There is a very easy way to come up with reliable estimate for the time needed for each activity when no past experience exists with such an activity. This method requires some understanding of the worst case value needed, the best case value, and the most probable value. We then use the formula below in Project Artifact 10 to calculate the estimated time needed for this particular activity. The formula is also applicable to cost estimates.

$$\text{Activity Time}_{\text{estimate}} = (\text{Worse case value} + (4 \times \text{Most probable value}) + \text{Best case value}) / 6$$

Project Artifact 10 Three-point formula to estimate time or cost of an activity.

A sample partial activity list is illustrated in Project Artifact 11.

Activity ID	WBS Parent	Activity Description	Duration (hrs)	Start	Finish	Dependency
1.1	5.1.1	Purchase ink	1	5/15/2008	5/15/2008	2.1
1.1	5.1.2	Purchase paper	1	5/15/2008	5/15/2008	2.1
2.1	6.1	Secure supplies funds	20	5/1/2008	5/10/2008	
3.1	2.2.3	Decide job, role, date format	0.5	5/15/2008	5/15/2008	
3.2	2.2.3	Decide accomplishments format	0.5	5/15/2008	5/15/2008	

Project Artifact 11 Sample partial activity list for a job hunting project.

Defining Resources

Many activities will require resources. Common resources for a job hunting project are software applications like word processors and spreadsheets to develop deliverables and artifacts; public transportation like subways, buses and airplanes to get to interviews; supplies like printer ink, paper, envelopes, stamps; services like cell phones Internet access, social networking, electronic faxing, and the list goes on. Some common questions to ask during resource definition are,

- How to categorize resources?
- What resources are needed to complete this activity?

- How long is the resource needed for?
- Is the resource shared, or do I have full control on it?
- What alternative resources are available?
- Are resources dependent on other resources?
- Are activities dependent on resources?
- Are dependencies one-to-one, one-to-many, many-to-many?
- What are the costs associated with these resources?
- Do resources have different performance levels?
- How will I travel to interviews?
- How will I retrieve information I need when I am away from home?
- How can I present past accomplishments to the interviewers?
- How can I print resumes at best value?
- How can I build strong networks?
- What do I need to maintain my networks?
- Who do I need as advisors?
- Who do I need as critiques?
- Who do I need as coaches?
- When do I need resources?
- How to reserve and book resources?

A useful project artifact to track resources to activities is called the project resource allocation matrix (RAM). It shows which resources are used for which activities. You can also add a column to your activity list and enter a resource for each activity on the project. A RAM is shown in Project Artifact 12.

Resource ID	Resource Name	Resource Description	Activity	Role
R1.1	Airline	Air travel to attend distant interviews	A6.7	Primary
R1.2	Subway	Local travel to attend urban interviews	A6.7	Secondary
R1.3	Personal Vehicle	Local travel to attend urban interviews Local travel to purchase supplies Local tracel to attend suburban interviews	A6.7 A9.8	Primary
R1.4	Rental Vehicle	Local travel to attend suburban interviews Remote travel to attend interviews	A6.7	Secondary Primary
R2.1	Laptop	To prepare resume To store resume	A10.5	Primary

Project Artifact 12 Sample partial RAM for a job hunting project.

Working on a Schedule

Once activities and resources and their dependencies are identified, a schedule for your job hunting should be prepared. Schedules could take many forms and shapes. Your schedule should be represented in a graphical format and should include on it the following pieces of information,

- Every activity on the project
- Every resource needed for each activity
- Dependency among activities
- Start and end dates for each activity
- Duration of activities

Chapter 7

Job Hunt Costs and Expenses

Cost Estimating, Cost Budgeting, Cost Control

إِنَّ الْمُبَذِّرِينَ كَانُواْ إِخْوَانَ الشَّيَاطِينِ وَكَانَ الشَّيْطَانُ لِرَبِّهِ كَفُورًا

Quran (17:27)

Behold, the squanderers are, indeed, of the ilk of the satans - inasmuch as Satan has indeed proved most ungrateful to his Sustainer.

Meaning of Quranic parable 27, chapter 17 (Al-Israa)

Estimating and Budgeting

Job hunting activities will require funding to implement and deploy. It is important to develop accurate estimates during the design phase so that you have a good idea of how long and how picky you can be in choosing opportunities and offers later in the deployment phase.

There are several approaches to estimating costs. Similar to activity duration estimation, costs can be estimated using the three point approach, through analogous comparison, bottom up estimating, or using rules of thumb.

Bottom up estimating is best for activities with limited details and large cost items because bottom up provides the highest accuracy and accounts for all details. For example, to estimate the cost to travel to attend a conference, you should estimate the air travel, hotel, conference fees, car rental, meals and other related expenses to interviewing, faxing, internet access, secure storage, and whatever else you think you might need to account.

I recall a few years ago while between projects, I took the opportunity to attend a conference for professional development. Although I was not planning on job hunting at the conference, I was interested in exploring potential consulting projects. I made sure I had my laptop and the ability to print resumes if needed. Although it might seem as a trivial activity, the cost to print a six page document away from your office or home could be high, if at all feasible, depending on where you are during your travel. If your conference is in a resort in a rural area 50 miles away from the nearest package shipping or business services office, it could easily cost you a hefty amount to print a few pages.

Some questions to ask during cost estimate and budgeting are,

- How much will the most cost for this activity possibly be, and what would the least be, and what is the most probable cost?
- What can possibly change to make the estimate for this activity dramatically increase of decrease?
- How many activities have pre-paid costs? What is the total amount of these pre-paid costs?
- What is the impact on the overall project if pre-paid activities could not be completed or executed?
- What alternatives exist to accomplish the activity at a lower cost?
- What alternatives exist to reuse resources or borrow resources instead of acquiring resources?
- What discounts, negotiation or promotions could apply to the cost of this activity?

Project Artifact 13 illustrates a sample cost estimate for few activities on a job hunting project related to the attendance of an out-of-town conference.

Activity ID	Cost	Activity Description	Cost Description
A6.7	$250	Travel to attend conference	RT tickets from DC to Orlando to attend the Conference on project mgmt
B2.1	$650	Attending project mgmt conference for a week	Conference fees
A6.8	$130	Local travel to attend urban interviews	Car rental in Orlando for one week while at conference
A10.5	$350	Lodging to attend conference	Lodging at an off-site hotel within 10 minutes from conference
A11.8	$2.50	Print copies of resume prior to travel locally in case printing is not feasible while traveling	Four copies of the 6-page resume at the local business center
A13.6	$300	Meals during the conference	Three meals per day for 7 days while on travel
A14.5	$100	Interview related	Extra cushion for other activities related to interviewing, not considered
Subtotal	$1,783		
H.10	$178	Cushion	Reserve for unexpected risks
Total	$1,961		Travel budget for conference

Project Artifact 13 Partial cost estimate for travel, meals and conference expenses.

A project or activity budget is the estimate for the cost of the project or activity in addition to a management reserve of some amount. It is the total approved funding for the project or activity defined.

Controlling Expenses

Without proper controls, it is very easy to overspend on a project, and in some cases, under spend. Both over and under spending are not healthy. A project that constantly exceeds its budget will soon run out of funds and be unable to sustain its costs and fail. A project that constantly spends less than budgeted might be delivering lower quality or partial deliverables than originally planned and expected. It is however very possible that a project spent less than budgeted and deliver exceptional quality deliverables as a result of its controls and practices.

Cost control is best achieved through the measurement of cost variance (CV), which is the difference between the earned value (EV) of the project or activity and the actual costs (AC) of the project or activity. This is indicated by the following formula presented in Project Artifact 14.

$$CV = EV - AC$$

Project Artifact 14 Cost variance for a project or activity.

EV is the value of the work completed to date on the project and is calculated as the percentage of work completed multiplied by the budget of the project at completion (BAC). AC is the actual costs spent on the project to date.

For the example in Project Artifact 15, if we assume that we completed the activities indicated for the costs shown, then our cost variance will be calculated as follows,

EV = BAC * % of work complete = $1961 * 1 = $1961

CV = $1961 - $2027 = -$66, which means the set of activities are over budget

Activity ID	Cost	Activity Description	Cost Description	Status	No of Hrs	AC
A6.7	$250	Travel to attend conference	RT tickets from DC to Orlando to attend the Conference on project mgmt	Completed	4	$320
B2.1	$650	Attending project mgmt conference for a week	Conference fees	Completed	40	$675
A6.8	$130	Local travel to attend urban interviews	Car rental in Orlando for one week while at conference	Completed	6	$105
A10.5	$350	Lodging to attend conference	Lodging at an off-site hotel within 10 minutes from conference	Completed	40	$345
A11.8	$2.50	Print copies of resume prior to travel locally in case printing is not feasible while traveling	Four copies of the 6-page resume at the local business center	Completed	1	$2
A13.6	$300	Meals during the conference	Three meals per day for 7 days while on travel	Completed	10.5	$260
A14.5	$100	Interview related	Extra cushion for other activities related to interviewing, not considered	Completed	4	$320
Subtotal	$1,783				106	$2,027
H.10	$178	Cushion	Reserve for unexpected risks	Not used		$0
Total	$1,961		Travel budget for conference			$2,027

Project Artifact 15 Estimated and budgeted costs along with actual costs.

The CV can be calculated at any point in the project. For example, if we calculated the CV at the time of arrival to Orlando, we can assume that only two activities are involved – A6.7 and A11.8. A6.7 is 50% complete as the activity is round trip travel, and since you are just arriving to Orlando, then 50% of A6.7 has been completed with an earned value of $125, in addition to the earned value of the hard copy resumes you have brought with you prior to leaving Washington as part of activity A11.8, which is another $2.5 in earned value. So, the total earned value at that point in time is $127.5 and the actual costs are $320 + $2 = $322 (assuming the airline return ticket is non-refundable, and not assuming that conference fees and hotel are pre-paid). The percent of work completed at this time is 2 hrs of south bound travel + 1 hr of resume copying = 3 hrs of a total 106 hrs.

Hence,
Percent of work completed = 3/106
BAC = 1961
EV = $55.5
AC = $322
Therefore, AC = $55.5 - $322 = -$266.5

It is clear that a cost variance report conducted on a regular basis can provide you with a good idea about the financial health of your project.

Chapter 8

Quality Hunts

Quality Planning, Quality Control

الَّذِينَ ضَلَّ سَعْيُهُمْ فِي الْحَيَاةِ الدُّنْيَا وَهُمْ يَحْسَبُونَ أَنَّهُمْ يُحْسِنُونَ صُنْعًا

Quran (18:104)

Those whose work and efforts have gone astray in this world's life, and who think that they are doing good work.

Meaning of Quranic parable 104, chapter 18 (The Cave)

Get What You Expect

Quality is defined as meeting the customer's expectations. In your job hunting, you have two main customers; you and the hiring manager. As a customer, your interests are in a job that meets the objectives and goals you defined in the scope statement. If you land a job that does not fully meet the scope statement, then you have not realized a quality job.

On the other hand, the hiring manager is a customer as well, expecting certain skills, experiences, and knowledge based on the opening needs, as advertised or communicated to you, and based on your response as presented in your resume.

When planning for quality on your job hunt project, you want to define key metrics to measure and compare to your customer's expectations at the time of project delivery.

Some questions to ask during quality planning as part of the design phase are,

- What should be my maximum response time to get back to an interviewer or recruiter?
- What should be the maximum length of my resume?
- What should be the minimum length of my resume?
- What attributes do I require in an interviewer and employer to accept an interview?
- What attributes do I require to attend a conference?
- What metrics will I use to assess the effectiveness of an interview?
- What metrics will I use to assess the effectiveness of my blog?
- How can I determine if my resume is at the highest possible quality?
- What metrics will I use to gauge how effective my networking is?
- How can I determine if my accomplishments portfolio is meetings its purpose?
- How can I determine the effectiveness of my cover letter?

To avoid quality problems, it is important that as part of quality assurance, both parties ensure that expectations are communicated clearly, accurately, and precisely. You should ask for a job description and fully understand the expectations of the employer, and vice versa.

Control Quality of the Results

To assess your quality, you will need to take measurements of the metrics you defined earlier as part of your quality planning. Quality control should occur throughout the project, but mostly once deliverables are available during the implementation and deployment phases.

Some measurements that could be used on your job hunt project are,

- Number of acronyms on the resume.
- Number of times I referred to my website during the interview.
- Number of times resume has been reviewed.

- Number of returned cold calls.
- Percentage of cold calls that turn into interviews.
- Average and median interview times.
- Rate of responses to openings for online, compared to mail.
- Number of questions raised by interviewer during meeting.
- Rate of misunderstandings on phone calls and interviews.
- Level of engagement of interviewer in the discussion.

Chapter 9

Job Hunt Soldiers

Building the Team, Manage Project Team

وَتَعَاوَنُواْ عَلَى الْبرِّ وَالتَّقْوَى وَلاَ تَعَاوَنُواْ عَلَى الإِثْمِ وَالْعُدْوَانِ

Quran (5:2)

And cooperate on righteousness and God-consciousness, and do not cooperate on evil and enmity.

Meaning of Quranic parable 2, chapter 5 (The Table)

Building Your Network Team

Your project team involves many people. Job hunting is not necessarily a 100% do it yourself project. You are definitely the project manager, main customer and stakeholder, and there are many other players in your project. Some roles that you will need on your project are,

- Subject matter experts
- Proofreaders
- Hiring managers
- Recruiters
- State employment agencies
- Career centers
- Professional organizations
- Colleagues
- Former manager and directors
- New contacts
- Others with similar interests

It is important to realize that as the project manager of your job hunting project, the control you have over your team is attained through motivation and coaching. More on both will be discussed in the communications chapter.

Table 14 summarizes the main roles and value that various team members could bring to the project.

Team Member	Value Offered	Example
Subject matter experts	Insights on industry trends, economic drivers, forecasts.	Your child's doctor could shed some light on challenges in patient medical history retrieval and how health care reform can make his office more efficient.
Proof reviewers	Review project deliverables.	A friend who has good English abilities and solid resume skills can proof review your resume.
Critiques	Review strategies, ideas, plans, project artifacts, deliverables.	Reviewing your scope statement with a coach.
Hiring managers	Insights on trends in interview process, selection and hiring.	A contact that you know who is a manager, even if at a different industry.
Recruiters	Supply / demand trends, compensation trends, industry trends.	A report on salaries or a phone call with a recruiter about latest changes over past month.
State employment agencies	Openings notices, search capabilities, data repositories, employer background checks, communication resources.	Local job agency can provide access to databases that are usually not accessible online, usage of facilities and could provide information about employers.
Career centers	Openings notices, search capabilities, data repositories, networking.	Centers at Universities and other professional groups offer email subscription services for notifications on potential opportunities.
Professional organizations	Openings notices, search capabilities, data repositories, networking, skills building, industry trends, knowledge acquisition.	Attending a workshop, or pursuing a professional certification.
Former managers and colleagues	Networking, supply / demand trends, compensation trends, industry trends, contracting opportunities, reference requests.	Reference letters.
New contacts	Networking, supply / demand trends, industry trends, contracting opportunities, potential ventures, opening announcements.	Joint project or contracting offers.
Others with similar interests	Lessons learned, experience building, barter services.	Learning from others experiences.
Family and friends	Emotional support, funding support	Investing in skills enhancement.

Table 14 Job hunting team members and areas of contribution.

Managing Your Team

To effectively manage your team, you need to be able to understand the motives for team members to be part of your project. Most people simply like to help out; just giving others the opportunity to help can be an incentive. You definitely need to include close friends and relatives on your job hunting team. Your team can assist with referrals, advice, feedback and opinions.

As long as you can reasonably control the time demand, the emotional support you expect, and keep your team informed; your team members will remain motivated to be part of your job hunt. It is very important to appreciate the time and efforts your team shares with you on your job hunting. If a friend has been helping you in critiquing your resume and forwarding you potential opportunities, then you should make sure to keep him or her informed on how your interviews are coming along.

Job Hunting Communications

Communications Planning, Information Distribution and Use, Manage Stakeholders

Chapter 10

وَاحْلُلْ عُقْدَةً مِّن لِّسَانِي يَفْقَهُوا قَوْلِي

Quran (20:25 – 20:26)

And loosen the know from my tongue so they may fully understand my speech

Meaning of Quranic parable 25-26, chapter 20 (Taha)

Communications is one of the most important areas of any project. The proper relaying of information across team members and stakeholders in a timely fashion is a key ingredient to project success.

How to Communicate

As part of your planning activities during the design phase, you should brainstorm and forecast the most effective communication throughout your project. Your findings will be documented in your job hunting communication management plan.

Some questions to ask during communications planning are,

- Who are my stakeholders?
- Who do I need to communicate with?
- How often do I need to communicate with the various stakeholders?
- What are the best approaches for communicating with my stakeholders?
- How can I store communication correspondence and retrieve it later?

- What formats are best suited for communicating different messages?
- What purposes do I have for communicating particular messages?
- How accurate, clear, precise, influential, relevant is my message to the other party?
- What technique is best suited to relay my message?
- How can coaching play a role in communicating with a stakeholder?
- What examples, illustrations, and elaboration can I apply to improve the clarity of my message?
- What details, specificity, and exactness can I include to improve the accuracy of my message?
- What validation and verification tactics can I apply to improve the precision of my message?
- How deep does my message or discussion need to be?
- How broad does my message or discussion need to be?
- What is the context and relationship of the other party to the discussion?
- How can I embed motivation, negotiation, and other influencing techniques to my discussion?
- How credible does my message appear from the other party's perspective?
- What logic am I using in my discussions?
- What evidence do I need to demonstrate to ensure the credibility of my point?
- When should I use the phone instead of email?
- When do social networking tools produce effective results?
- What items are non-negotiable?

Using and Retrieving Information

To use information, it must be in a format that is easy to understand and utilize in decision-making. This can be accomplished through various means depending on the type of information and decision to be made.

You will need to organize your job hunting information through categorizing and classifying various pieces of information. For example, one category could be project deliverables information, and another could be project artifacts information. The former category will focus on information things like your resume versions, types, uses, attributes and other deliverables of your project. The latter will focus more on project performance, deliverable quality measures, cost and schedule variance, risk measures and other aspects of the project itself through the use of reports.

Several reports are shown below in Project Artifact 16 through Project Artifact 18. Issue logs are useful in tracking open items that need resolution and could potentially turn into problems. Productivity reports are helpful in tracking progress and planning for future changes. Lessons learned capture experiences for planning purposes. Some experiences might be then turned into issues and appear on the issues log, while others might just be kept in the lessons learned for potential future use.

Issue ID	Issue Title	Description	Impact Level (1 - 5)	Date Detected	Resolution Plan	Current Status
1	No reponses	Applied to 20 positions over two weeks ago, and have not heard back from a single contact that application was received	5	6/1/2008	6/7: Shared resume with three team members, all agree resume is very solid and an eye grabber. Need to check for diverse sources of opportunities. 6/5: Review the application method, opportunity identification method, resume size, resume attractiveness	Open
...						

Project Artifact 16 Sample issue log.

Work ID	Work Item	Accomplishment	Date	Next Steps	Current Status
1	Develop resume for University medical centers	Tailored the general hospital resume to be more fit for University hospitals	6/15/2008	Review resume for spelling mistakes	In Progress

Project Artifact 17 Sample weekly productivity report.

Exp ID	Experience	Expectation	Date	Suggested Actions	Current Status
1	Recruiter mentioned resume is too short	I expected a resume of two pages to be the right size. Most recruiters in the past asked for a two page resume and few asked for three pages, but no one seemed to expect a long resume.	7/1/2008	Discuss with some hiring managers and share resume.	In Progress

Project Artifact 18 Sample lessons learned report.

Managing Your Stakeholders

Coaching is a powerful technique for managing your team. Coaching is a function where one can help other team members learn new knowledge, skills, and experiences to take on more responsibilities. In the case of your project, the function of coaching is to help your team members better understand your position, needs, challenges, and to assist them in taking a role on your job hunting project.

Good coaching conversations requires several attributes to be successful, which are,

- Mutual – Both parties need to be able to listen and talk.
- Change oriented – Focus has to be on future outcomes with the intention to introduce some change.
- Respect and trust – Both need to be communicated through opinion sharing, questions, listening and serious thought.
- Process based – There has to be clear goals, milestones and a plan.
- Listening skills – Parties have to be attending, acknowledging, querying, reflecting, indicating respect, and able to recap the discussion in a form of a summary
- Immediacy – Parties need to be interested and willing in the conversation.

Negotiation is common on job hunting projects, especially when it comes to discussing offers. Negotiation is an iterative communication process for the purpose of reaching a joint agreement about differing needs or ideas. It is important when negotiating to create a win-win environment with strong rapport, clearly understand the other party's position, ask plenty of questions, apply coaching concepts, be credible, and find common ground.

Negotiation goes through several main stages, summarized as,

- Orientation – Getting familiar with the other party's interests.
- Research – Collecting more facts, root causes for interests, dependencies, constraints, and areas of flexibility.
- Alternatives planning – Defining alternative proposals and offerings.
- Resistance – Meeting with other party and addressing points of disagreement.

- Reformulation – Introducing the points of discussion from a different perspective with defined common ground, and elaborating on differences of position.
- Bargaining – Making offers to the other party to close an agreement.
- Decision-making – Reaching a final decision.

Typically things that could be negotiated are compensation, start dates, responsibilities, working hours, bonuses, and titles.

As a strong project manager, you need to keep your team motivated. Motivation is keeping your team involved and energized to take some action with a specific direction in mind. Motivated team members will be patient and persistent.

The following points are useful in motivating self and other team members,

- Communicate is same language and concepts.
- Understand other people's position.
- Explain what's in it for them.
- Solicit feedback and ideas.
- Share goals, vision and plans.
- Inspire trust and loyalty

Project Risk Management

Risk Management Planning, Risk Identification, Qualitative Analysis, Quantitative Analysis, Risk Response Planning, Risk Monitoring, and Control

Chapter 11

إِذْ أَوْحَيْنَا إِلَى أُمِّكَ مَا يُوحَى
أَنِ اقْذِفِيهِ فِي التَّابُوتِ فَاقْذِفِيهِ فِي الْيَمِّ فَلْيُلْقِهِ الْيَمُّ
بِالسَّاحِلِ يَأْخُذْهُ عَدُوٌّ لِّي وَعَدُوٌّ لَّهُ وَأَلْقَيْتُ عَلَيْكَ
مَحَبَّةً مِّنِّي وَلِتُصْنَعَ عَلَى عَيْنِي

Quran (20:38-20:39)

When We inspired your mother (Oh, Moses) with this inspiration. Place him in a chest and throw it into the river, and thereupon the river will cast him ashore, (and) one who is an enemy unto Me and an enemy unto him will adopt him. "And (thus early) I spread Mine Own love over you - and (this) in order that thou might be formed under Mine eye.

Meaning of Quranic parable 38-39, chapter 20 (Taha)

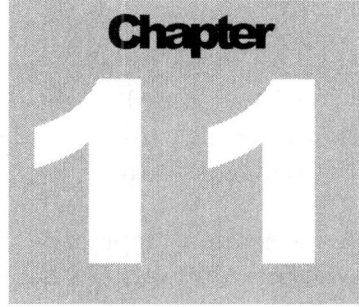

What Can Go Wrong

Dozens of things can go wrong on your job hunting project, so risk planning should start as early as the concept phase. Risk planning involves defining how to identify risk, how to qualify them, prioritization of the risks, and responding to them.

Some common approaches for risk identification involve interviewing others who passed through similar experiences of job hunting, interviewing team members, forecasting what-if scenarios, sketching flow charts and conducting strength, weakness, opportunity, and threat analysis (SWOT).

Common job hunting risks,

- Delays in getting to interviews due to traffic congestion.
- Hiring manager out of office on the day of the interview.
- Severe weather.
- Online resume submission not reaching a human.
- Online job announcements outdated.
- Not enough time to apply to a position prior to a deadline.
- Getting lost on the way to an interview.
- Perceived as overqualified for a position.
- Employer's staff too busy on the interview day and meet you much later than agreed upon time.
- Asked to give an overview of self on the spot when not prepared.
- Asked inappropriate questions at an interview.
- Employer gets back to you after a very long time when you are out of town for two weeks for vacation.
- Job offer is too low for your experiences and position responsibilities.
- Interviewer is influenced by past interviewees creating false impressions.

Qualifying the Risks

As you plan your project, you will compile a list of risks. You might come up with a large number of risks, which then need to be qualified. The qualification process occurs by analyzing the probability of occurrence and impact of occurrence of each risk.

As part of risk management, you need to define what is considered a low, medium, and high risk. The value for the threshold of each is defined as part of your risk management plan. For example you might decide that risk that impact the project by more than $100 are medium, and those higher than $500 are high.

Examples of parameters to consider when deciding on the impact level of a risk are,

- Level of ease of finding the opportunity
- Reputation of employer
- Long term employment benefits at employer
- Distance to the interview
- Number of interviewers meeting in a single meeting
- Size of resume
- Number of revisions of a resume
- Size and duration of portfolio slide show

A qualified risk list is a smaller number of risks that you will manage and track on your project. All other risks will just be accepted, meaning that you will accept the outcomes should they occur and become problems.

Risk ID	Risk	Impact	Date Identified	Response Plan	Current Status
1	Interviewer comes to meeting late	Interview could be cut short no leaving enough time to present self well, or meeting might extend late impacting later interview across the town.	7/1/2008	Have a short slide show ready in case we run short on time to show it in 2-4 minutes before leaving, and leave printed copy with interviewer. Push back second interview start time 1 hr to give enough time.	Mitigated

Project Artifact 19 Sample risk register.

Prioritizing the Risks

Calculating the risk value allows us to rank risks. Risk value is calculated as the product of the risk impact in dollar amounts and the risk probability of occurrence. Project Artifact 20 provides a sample of three risk and their priority levels.

Risk ID	Risk	Impact (Low < 0.1, 0.1< Med <0.5, 0.5 < High)	Probability (Low < 0.1, 0.1< Med <0.5, 0.5 < High)	Risk Value
2	Flat tire on way to interview	0.75	0.25	0.1875
1	Interviewer comes to meeting late	0.75	0.5	0.375
3	Interviewer does not have copy of resume	0.75	0.85	0.6375

Project Artifact 20 Sample list of prioritized risks.

Responding to Risks

There are various approaches in responding to risks such as acceptance, mitigation, and transfer. Accepting a risk is to do nothing to respond to it and just accept the consequences whenever they occur, this could be a good approach when risk impacts are very low and probability of occurrence are not high. Mitigation of risks occurs when the amount of rework associated with the consequences of a risk occurrence or the impact cannot be ignored. Mitigation involves workarounds, backup plans, and simplification of deliverables or processes. Transfer of risk involves its move to another entity. Project Artifact 21 illustrates sample risks and the mitigation approach used.

Risk ID	Risk	Mitigation Approach
2	Flat tire on way to interview	Transfer / Mitigation: Use metro instead of car
1	Interviewer comes to meeting late	Mitigation: Remind interviewer of our meeting ahead of time
3	Interviewer does not have copy of resume	Mitigation: Take two extra copies with me
4	Resume has one typo and no time to correct before deadline	Acceptance: Submit resume anyway, there will be no other chance to apply

Project Artifact 21 Sample job hunting risk mitigation scenarios.

Appendix A

Acronyms

AC	Actual Cost
ASQ	American Society of Quality
BAC	Budget at Completion
CPI	Cost Performance Index
CSEP	Certified Systems Engineering Professional
CV	Cost Variance
ETC	Estimate to Complete
EV	Earned Value
IEEE	Institute of Electrical and Electronics Engineers
PMI	Project Management Institute
PMP	Project Management Professional
PV	Planned Value
RAM	Role Assignment Matrix
SOW	Statement of Work
WBS	Work breakdown structure

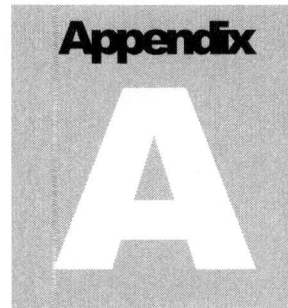

Appendix B

Bibliography

Joseph Devito, "Essentials of Human Communication", 2nd Edition, Harpers Collins, 1995.

Ayman Nassar, "Principles of Project Management: In 3 Hrs", Intercontinental Networks, Feb 2009.

"A Guide to the Project Management Body of Knowledge", Third Edition, Project Management Institute, 2004.

Kathleen Romero, "Addressing Tough Issues Through Ethical Analysis", PMI Today, Project Management Institute, December 2008.

Frederick Ball, Barbara Ball, "Killer Interviews", McGraw Hill, 1996.

Lee Miller, "Get More Money on Your Next Job: 25 Proven Strategies for Getting More Money, Better Benefits and Greater Job Security", McGraw Hill, 1998.

Susan Whitcomb, "Job Search Magic", Jist Works, 2006.

Holy Quran, compiled on the narration of Hafs Bin Solyman Ibn Al-Moghera Al-Asady Al-Kufy for the recitation of Asim Bin Abi-Al-Najood Al-Kufy Al-Taby based on Abi-Abdelrahman Abdellah Bin Habib Al-Solmy based on Othman Bin Affan and Ali Bin Abi-Talib and Zaid Bin-Thabit and Abi-Bin-Kaab based on the Prophet Muhammad (peace be upon him).

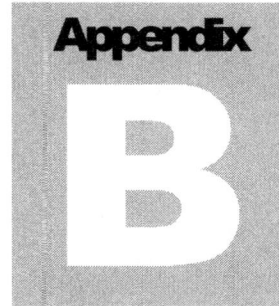

Appendix C

Practice Sheets

1. How is your job hunt unique, and why? Critically compare it to previous job hunts, others currently looking for a job.

2. What are your start and end target dates?

3. What major risks and uncertainties do you anticipate?

4. What are your final job hunt project deliverables? List at least five.

5. Give yourself a statement of work for your job hunt project.

6. What is your career or life vision?

7. What is your career or life mission?

8. Develop your job hunt project vision and mission.

   a. Vision

   b. Mission

9. How many phases will define your job hunt project, and why?

10. Sketch the level of activity of your planning and control processes for each phase on your job hunting project.

11. What are some economic factors affecting your job hunt and their impact levels?

12. What are some major trends that could affect your job hunt? How do these trends affect your project?

13. State your project charter.

14. How will you ensure that you remain focused on your job hunting project? Outline any plans in detail.

15. Develop your job hunt scope statement.

16. Draft the outline of your cost management plan, risk management plan, communications management plan and time utilization management plan for your project.

17. List and draft the layout of four control reports you can use to stay on track with your project.

18. Sketch a WBS for your project. Show at least 3 levels of detail.

19. List at least 5 time killers you exhibit on your project, and list approaches of addressing them.

Time Killer	Approach to Address

20. List at least 4 time boosters you exhibit on your project, and why they are effective.

Time Boosters	Effectiveness Cause

21. Define at least three activities on your project and map them to work items in your WBS.

22. Define at the resources associated with the activities define in 21.

23. Estimate the cost for each of the activities in 21, and the associated resources identified in 22.

24. Identify three deliverables and at least 3 metrics to assess each project deliverable.

25. List four team members of your project, which group do they belong to and how can you leverage their experiences on your project?

26. How will you communicate with your identified team members in 25 and how frequently?

27. Identify 5 risks on your project, and explain why they are considered risks.

Risk	Rationale

28. What are the main components of your risk management plan?

29. Sketch a risk probability-impact matrix to show the location of each risk.

30. Explain how you will respond to these risks to eliminate or minimize their presence.

Risk	Response Plan

31. Sketch your probability – impact matrix after the first iteration of your response plan.

Appendix D

Tips for the Recession

… and other times as well

While Still Employed

1. Volunteer ideas for improvement to the boss. Do not fear that your scope of work will increase and the due date will stay the same, affecting how your work performance will be perceived. It is always good to constantly get more work added to your plate. It shows commitment, initiative and ensures that you will be busy. After all it's the right thing to do.
2. Extend your reach. Offer to help in other departments. Volunteer a couple of hours to help a different group on a project they are working on without charging it to your department. Work with groups that are testing out new services or products.
3. Be a good sales person. Although there might be a sales department, and sales staff who get paid salaries and commissions to make that deal. It is in everyone's interest in the organization to sell the products or services the organization offers. Make sure to capture leads and communicate them to your sales group, be an ambassador to your company and promote its brand, products and values.
4. Connect with the leadership and the folks in the field. Stay on top of events and opportunities, as well as threats by communicating with others at various vertical levels and not just your peers or those you work with on a daily basis.
5. Learn and teach. Learn on the job, learn from experiences, learn from others, learn from training, learn from books and teach others.
6. Participate in conferences, share opinions on blogs and other professional meetings.
7. Network and update your network. Do not let your network list get obsolete. Make sure to stay in touch and up to date with your contacts.

8. Develop status reports for yourself, even if the boss does not ask for them. Weekly are best, monthly are also useful, if you can not do weekly reports. They will help when you need to update your resume every six months. You also never know when your boss might be leaving the company and you might get a new one, who does not know too much about your performance and accomplishments.
9. If you know a layoff is coming negotiate with your employer for some extra benefits, examples are company phones, discounted laptops, office furniture, club memberships, prorated bonuses, paid training and anything else that helps you get employed quicker.

After Losing Your Job or After Graduation

1. Stay busy. Split your time between applying the approach mentioned in this book and working. Even though you do not have a job, you can volunteer at local non-profits offering services in your domain. It will provide you with contacts and make you stay focused and energized.
2. Seize the opportunity. Being laid off is the perfect time to catch up on the scare hours spent with the kids, or spouse. It is the great opportunity to work remotely while you travel or visit out-of-town relatives. You can research new regions and even countries.
3. Be innovative. Look for skills that you have that can be redeployed in a different format. An engineer can easily teach algebra and calculus to high school kids at the public library. Seek ways to use technology and the Internet to promote your professional brand.
4. Get up to date. When we work 8-5 every day we become too confined into our one tiny areas of focus. Meet new people, establish contacts with younger generations to learn new tools and technologies, and connect with older generations to learn experiences and gain connections.
5. Seek a mentor. Attend workshops like the one I offer on pragmatic job hunting, and stay in touch with the instructor. I often come across opportunities that could suit some of my workshop participants. In some cases I could even connect participants with each other allowing them to form a strong complementing team.
6. Plan carefully and don't panic. We can not think under stress, and if we do, our thinking is irrational and unrealistic. Make sure you get enough rest and you plan and research enough before you take actual steps in seeking a job.

7. Invest in you capabilities. Make sure you are up to date on the subject matter of your domain. Acquire technology, tools and skills needed to give you a boost. Many of these resources can be acquired for free or very low cost.

Appendix E

A Word on Interviews

Phone Interviews

1. Smile. Although the interviewer can not see you, a smile will provide a positive tone and will make the interviewer feel you are more personable and interested in the position.
2. No PJs. Do not crawl out of bed to the phone interview. Make sure you have been awake for at least an hour before the interview and that you have been talking for at least 10 minutes before you get on the phone. The last thing you want on the interview is to shorten it because the interviewer can not understand your vice.
3. Speak slower and clearer than usual. You want to make sure your voice is understood and reflects confidence.
4. Choose a quiet location. A radio or television in a nearby room might not be a distraction to you, but it might be very audible and distracting to the interviewer; same applies to children and pets.

In-Person Interviews

1. Dress formally. When in doubt over dress rather than appear unprofessional.
2. Present your portfolio. Make sure to have a simple and concise portfolio to present. It could be in paper format, or an electronic presentation.
3. Promote your brand. Highlight and clarify what distinguishes you from the crowd.
4. Show interest. Ask if you can take a tour in the facility, ask if you can meet others that you might be working with.

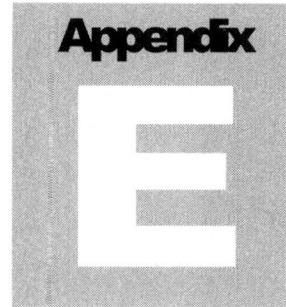

Notes

Index

Accomplishments 8, 29, 32, 37, 39, 62, 71, 109
Activity Planning 47
Activity Time................................ 61
Actual Costs 67, 68
Advisors 62
Bios.. 37
Blogs 9, 38
Brainstorming 48
Budget 20, 49, 66, 67
Certifications 37, 39
Change Control 28, 30, 50
Charter ... 19, 24, 25, 26, 27, 31, 45, 46, 53, 55, 96
Charter 27, 31, 46
Closing Processes 25, 35, 41, 52
Coaches 62
Coaching 81
Compensation.... 18, 24, 27, 29, 43, 55, 82
Concept.. 22, 23, 31, 46, 47, 49, 51, 53
Conference Calls......................... 37
Conferences......... 7, 25, 38, 40, 108
Consequences 86
Constraints 28, 47, 49, 55, 81
Control Processes...........25, 29, 52
Controlling 19, 45, 49, 50, 66
Cost ..20, 23, 26, 27, 28, 29, 32, 33, 46, 47, 50, 51, 61, 64, 65, 66, 67, 69, 80, 97, 102, 110
Cost Control....................36, 39, 67
Cost Variance 67
Cover Letters......................... 37, 39
Critical Thinking......................... 38
Critiques 62
Decompose 56
Deliverables..15, 16, 20, 22, 25, 26, 29, 34, 36, 37, 38, 39, 40, 41, 43, 46, 47, 48, 49, 50, 51, 52, 57, 61, 66, 71, 79, 86, 93, 102
Directing 19
Earned Value.......................... 67, 68
Employment Agreements 40, 43
Estimation 34, 60
Execution......20, 29, 35, 36, 38, 41, 48, 50
Face-Face Meetings.............. 38, 40
Follow Up Lists 40, 43
Forecasts 19, 23
Initiation 19, 25, 41, 45
Life Cycle 23, 50
Management.............................. 19,
Management Reserve................. 66
Milestones......23, 28, 35, 38, 55, 81
Mission..... 8, 19, 20, 24, 31, 32, 52, 56, 94
Mitigation.................................... 86
Negotiation......................38, 40, 81
Network Lists........................ 37, 39
Offer Letters 40, 43
Organizing 19
Phase 22, 23, 24, 25, 26, 27, 28, 29, 30, 31, 32, 33, 34, 35, 36, 38, 39, 40, 41, 42, 43, 45, 47, 48, 50, 51, 52, 53, 54, 55, 64, 71, 78, 84, 95
Planning. 19, 26, 27, 33, 36, 39, 45, 47, 48, 70, 78, 83
Planning Processes............... 25, 47
Positioning.........................8, 24, 49
Prioritization 34
Professional Events.................... 38
Publications 37, 39, 40
Quality.................32, 34, 37, 70, 71
Registered Events................. 37, 39
Research..... 12, 16, 24, 28, 30, 109, 110
Resource Allocation Matrix 62

Resource Planning........................ 47
Responses................................37, 39
Resumes..................................37, 39
Risk...15, 23, 26, 32, 33, 37, 39, 46, 48, 50, 51, 80, 84, 85, 86, 97, 104, 106
Risk...16, 32, 36, 37, 39, 40, 83, 84, 85, 104, 106
Scenarios.............19, 23, 24, 84, 86
Schedule..16, 34, 36, 37, 39, 60, 63
Scope 20, 25, 26, 27, 28, 29, 30, 31, 32, 33, 45, 46, 47, 49, 50, 51, 54, 55, 56, 57, 58, 59, 70, 97, 108
Scope Statement....... 28, 55, 56, 70
Stakeholder..............................36, 39
Statement Of Work.........18, 50, 93
Status Reports...28, 37, 39, 51, 109
Strategic Thinking.................... 7, 48
Systems......................... 2, 11, 12, 29
Target Employers..................37, 39
Trends.....16, 24, 25, 28, 31, 34, 96
Vision.....19, 20, 24, 25, 31, 52, 56, 82, 93, 94,
WBS............. *See* Work Breakdown Structure
Work.10, 15, 16, 19, 22, 23, 24, 26, 28, 29, 30, 33, 35, 38, 41, 45, 47, 48, 49, 50, 51, 54, 55, 56, 57, 58, 60, 67, 68, 70, 101, 108, 109
Work Breakdown Structure 34, 37, 40, 88
Work Performance................36, 38

www.ingramcontent.com/pod-product-compliance
Lightning Source LLC
Chambersburg PA
CBHW051414200326
41520CB00023B/7227